YONDE KAITE

よんでかいて

JAPANESE WORKBOOK

PRIMARY LEVEL 4

WRITTEN BY

ANNE RAJAKUMAR

WITH ORIGINAL ILLUSTRATIONS BY

JENNIFER CHENG

First published in 1999, reprinted in 2002, 2007, 2008, 2010, 2012, 2013, 2014, 2015
This redesigned edition first published in 2017, reprinted in 2020, 2021, 2022, 2023.

Insight Publications Pty Ltd
3/350 Charman Road
Cheltenham Victoria 3192
Australia

Tel: +61 3 8571 4950
Fax: +61 3 8571 0257
Email: books@insightpublications.com.au

www.insightpublications.com.au

ISBN: 9781875882229

Illustrations by Jennifer Cheng; other images courtesy of Shutterstock
Cover and internal design by Gisela Beer
Proofing by Sage Napthine-Morrison and Fabrice Wilmann

Printed by Markono Print Media Pte Ltd

Author acknowledgements
Special thanks to my family, Kumar, Timothy and Jessica, for their constant support and assistance and to Barbara and Chris for their untiring advice and unwavering encouragement and help.

Table of Contents

LANGUAGE AND EXTENSION LESSONS

Lesson 1 ME 5
Lesson 2 QUESTIONS AND ANSWERS 7
Lesson 3 THE WORLD 9
Lesson 4 WHERE DO YOU LIVE? 11
Lesson 5 NUMBERS 1 – 50 13
Lesson 6 NUMBERS 51 – 100 15
Lesson 7 CLASSROOM INSTRUCTIONS 17
Lesson 8 MONTHS OF THE YEAR 19
Lesson 9 SEASONS 21
Lesson 10 ABOUT THE SEASONS 23
Lesson 11 MAKING QUESTIONS 25
Lesson 12 YES OR NO 27
Lesson 13 FAST FOOD 29
Lesson 14 DRINKS 31
Lesson 15 TABLE MANNERS 33
Lesson 16 THIS OR THAT? 35
Lesson 17 WHAT IS THIS OR THAT? 37
Lesson 18 PLACES TO GO 39
Lesson 19 GOING PLACES 41
Lesson 20 GOING PLACES SENTENCES 43

WRITING LESSONS AND WORKSHEETS

Lesson 1 HIRAGANA: SMALL TSU 45
Lesson 2 HIRAGANA: LONG O 47
Lesson 3 HIRAGANA: PARTICLES WA AND E 49
Lesson 4 HIRAGANA BLENDS: KYA KYU KYO 51
Lesson 5 HIRAGANA BLENDS: GYA GYU GYO 53
Lesson 6 HIRAGANA BLENDS: SHA SHU SHO 55
Lesson 7 HIRAGANA BLENDS: JA JU JO 57
Lesson 8 HIRAGANA BLENDS: CHA CHU CHO 59
Lesson 9 HIRAGANA BLENDS: NYA NYU NYO 61
Lesson 10 HIRAGANA BLENDS: HYA HYU HYO 63
Lesson 11 HIRAGANA BLENDS: BYA BYU BYO 65
Lesson 12 HIRAGANA BLENDS: PYA PYU PYO 67
Lesson 13 HIRAGANA BLENDS: MYA MYU MYO 69
Lesson 14 HIRAGANA BLENDS: RYA RYU RYO 71

REVISION LESSONS 73

ASSESSMENT LESSONS 77

WORDLIST 81

HIRAGANA CHART 86

日本語

はじめまして。	I'm pleased to meet you.
☺☺☺ です。	I am ☺☺☺.
☺☺☺ に すんでいます。	I live in ☺☺☺.
そして	and also
☺☺☺ さい です。	I am ☺☺☺ years old.
ことし（は）	this year
☺☺☺ ねんせい です。	I am in grade ☺☺☺.
どうぞ よろしく。	a greeting used after introducing oneself

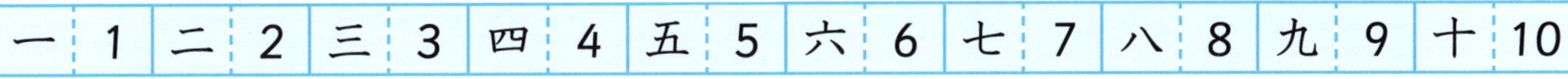

一	1	二	2	三	3	四	4	五	5	六	6	七	7	八	8	九	9	十	10

Trace over the Japanese words, then fill in the blank boxes with information about yourself.

THE SELF-INTRODUCTION RAP

はじめまして [ ] です。

That's my name, as you can guess.

[ ] に すんでいます。

Won't you come and visit us?

そして [ ] さい です。

That's my age. Yes! Yes! Yes!

ことし は、[ ] ねんせいです。

That's the grade that I like best!

どうぞ よろしく。

That's the way I introduce myself to you!

はじめまして。	I'm pleased to meet you.
☺☺☺ です。	I am ☺☺☺.
☺☺☺ に すんでいます。	I live in ☺☺☺.
そして	and also
☺☺☺ さい です。	I am ☺☺☺ years old.
ことし (は)	this year
☺☺☺ ねんせい です。	I am in grade ☺☺☺.
どうぞ よろしく。	a greeting used after introducing oneself

一	1	二	2	三	3	四	4	五	5	六	6	七	7	八	8	九	9	十	10

Trace over the hiragana letters and fill in the blank boxes to complete the self-introduction rap.

☐☐☐☐☐☐ ☐ です。

That's my name as you can guess.

☐ に ☐☐☐☐☐☐☐

Won't you come and visit us?

☐☐☐ ☐ さい ☐☐☐

That's my age. Yes! Yes! Yes!

ことし は、☐☐☐☐☐ です。

That's the grade that I like best!

☐☐☐ ☐☐☐☐。

That's the way I introduce myself to you!

Use the Japanese sentences from the self-introduction rap to write your own self introduction in Japanese. Don't leave any spaces between words but do end your sentences with a full stop in its own box, like this: 。. When you come to the end of a row you may break your word and continue on to the next row. Use one box for each letter when you use English words.

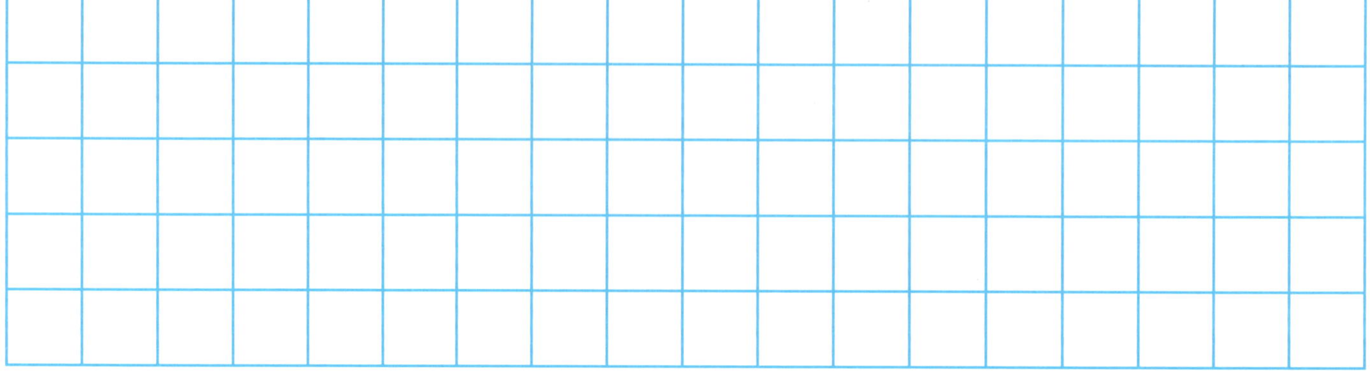

おなまえ は なん です か。	What's your name?
どこ に すんでいます か。	Where do you live?
なん さい です か。	How old are you?
なん ねんせい です か。	What grade are you in?

ぼく は ☺☺☺ です。	I am ☺☺☺. (boys)
わたし は ☺☺☺ です。	I am ☺☺☺. (girls)
☺☺☺ に すんでいます。	I live in ☺☺☺.
☺☺☺ さい です。	I am ☺☺☺ years old.
☺☺☺ ねんせい です。	I am in grade ☺☺☺.

なまえ is the Japanese word for 'name', but when you talk about someone else's name you must add the respectful prefix お to the word なまえ, thus:
なまえ → おなまえ
name (your) name

どこ Where?

なん What?

一	1	二	2	三	3	四	4	五	5	六	6	七	7	八	8	九	9	十	10

Trace over the Japanese sentences, then join the matching questions and answers with a line. There are spaces in the Japanese sentences to make them easier to read.

なん ねんせい です か。　　とうきょう に すんでいます。
どこ に すんでいます か。　　わたし は はな です。
おなまえ は なん です か。　　四ねんせい です。
なん さい です か。　　九さい です。

Trace over the Japanese letters, then fill in the blank boxes to complete the dialogue. Make your own dialogue using the two blank speech boxes. Draw pictures of your characters in the frames.

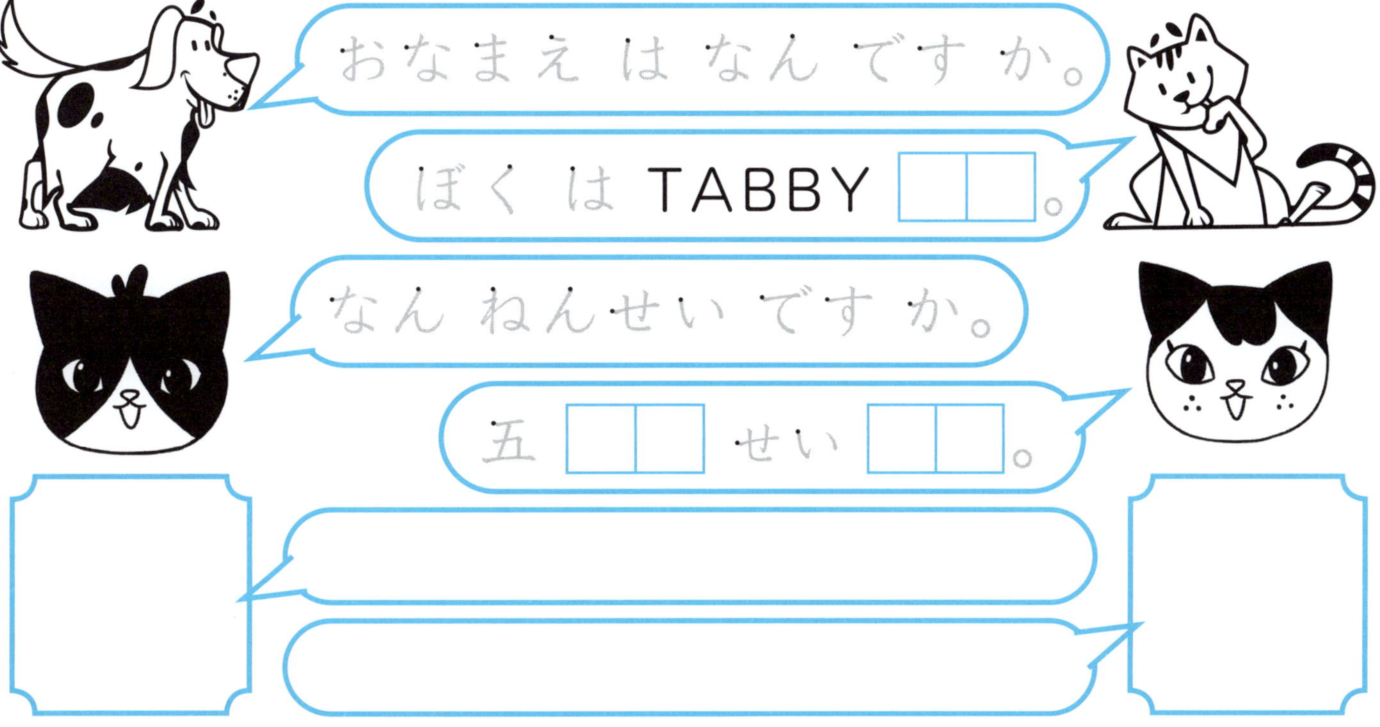

おなまえ は なん です か。	What's your name?
どこ に すんでいます か。	Where do you live?
なん さい です か。	How old are you?
なん ねんせい です か。	What grade are you in?

ぼく は ☺☺☺ です。	I am ☺☺☺. (boys)
わたし は ☺☺☺ です。	I am ☺☺☺. (girls)
☺☺☺ に すんでいます。	I live in ☺☺☺.
☺☺☺ さい です。	I am ☺☺☺ years old.
☺☺☺ ねんせい です。	I am in grade ☺☺☺.

一	1	二	2	三	3	四	4	五	5	六	6	七	7	八	8	九	9	十	10

Meet Hana (はな) and Tim. はな is from Japan. Tim lives in Perth. He is in grade 4 and is 9 years old. This is what happened when はな came to visit Tim's school. はな asked Tim lots of questions. Fill in the blank boxes to complete Tim's replies. Use one box for each romaji letter.

おなまえ は なん です か。

どこ に すんでいます か。

なん さい です か。

なん ねんせい です か。

Trace over the Japanese names of the parts of the world.

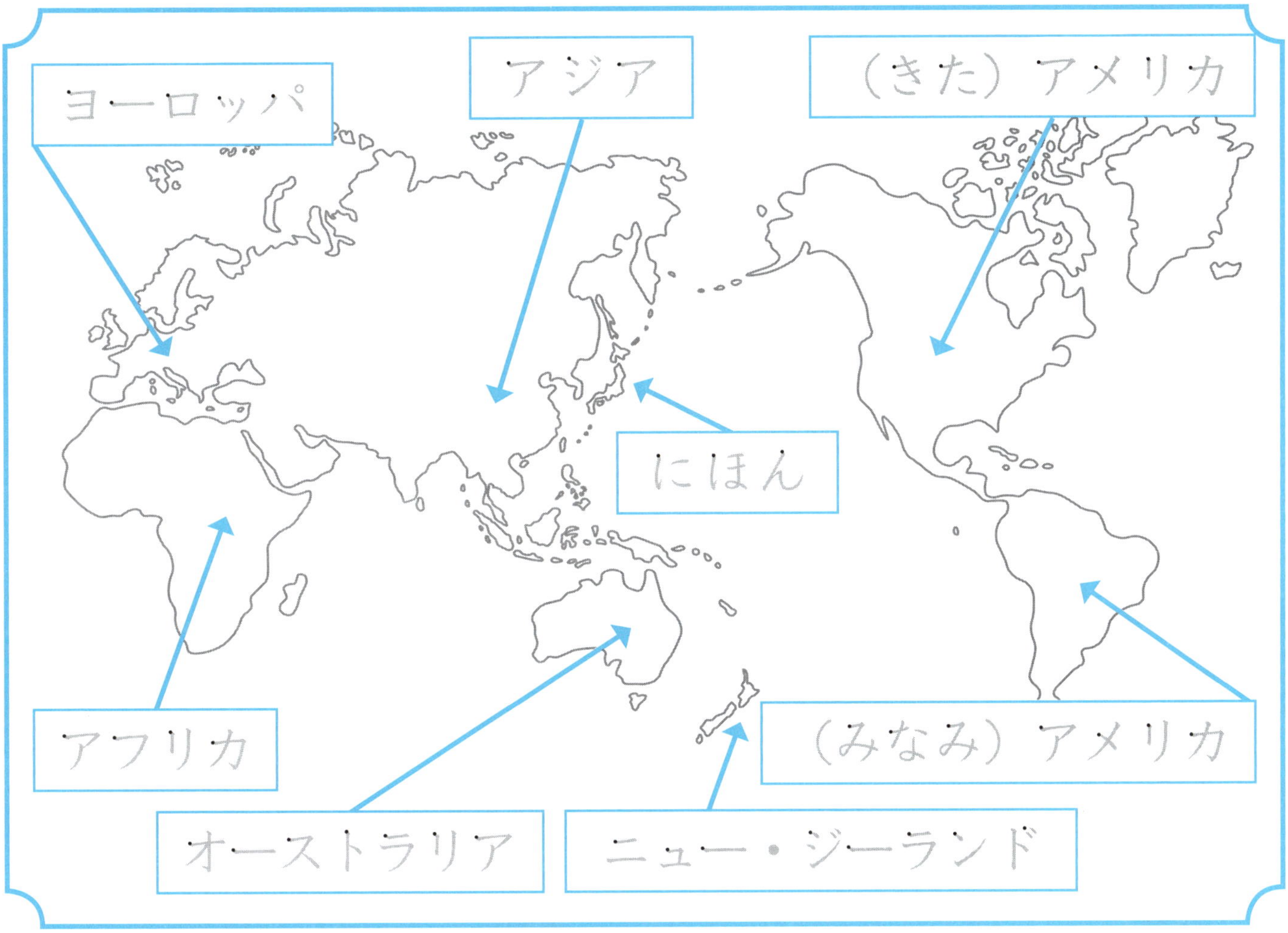

ヨーロッパ

アジア

（きた）アメリカ

にほん

アフリカ

（みなみ）アメリカ

オーストラリア

ニュー・ジーランド

Write the names of these places in Japanese.

一 Africa
二 Asia
三 Australia
四 Europe
五 Japan
六 New Zealand
七 North America
八 South America

Look at the Japanese place names. Insert them into the correct boxes on the map using hiragana letters. Can you do it from memory?

にほん	Japan
しこく	Shikoku
おおさか	Osaka
ほっかいどう	Hokkaido

とうきょう	Tokyo
きゅうしゅう	Kyushu
ほんしゅう	Honshu

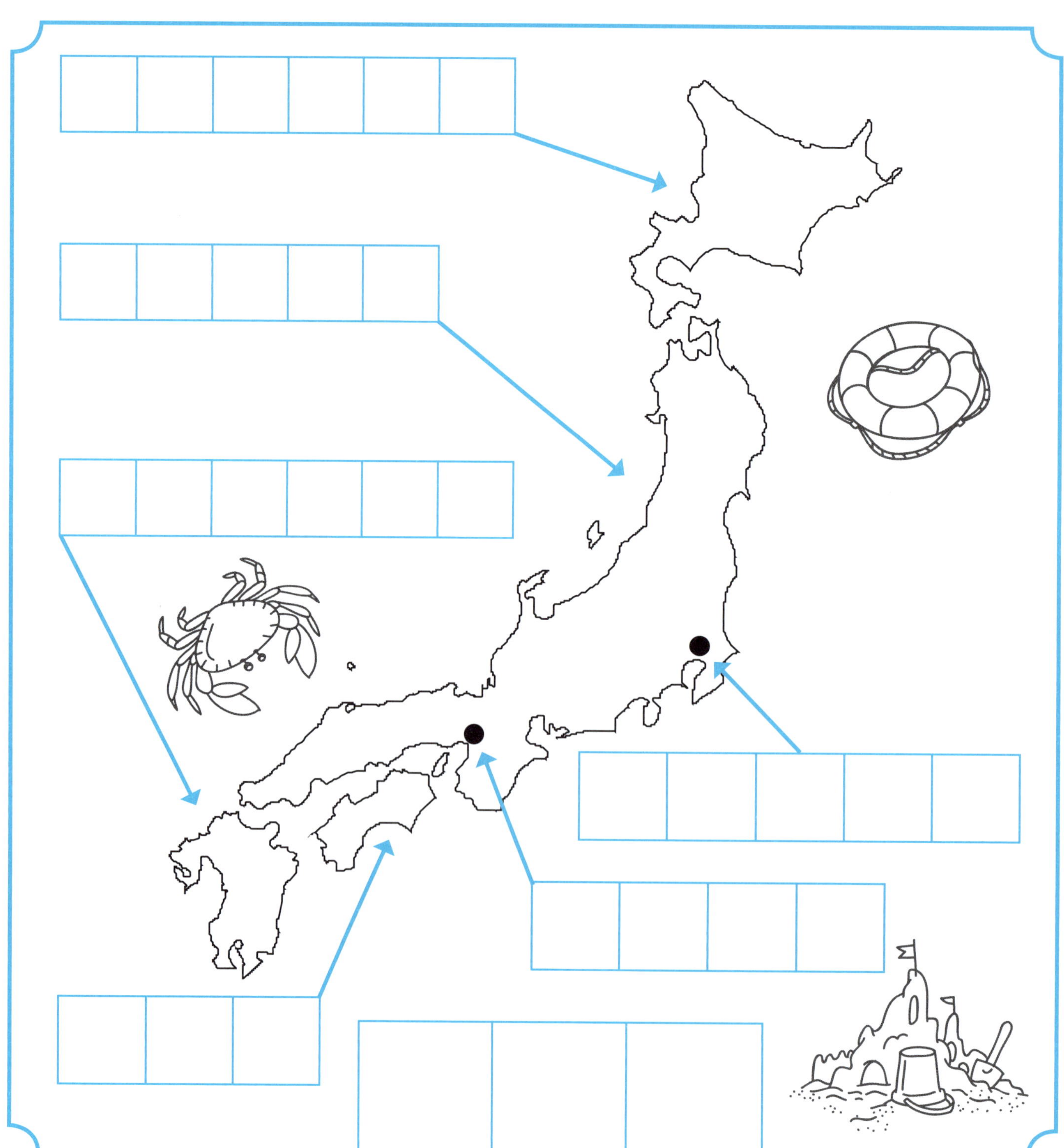

アフリカ	Africa
アジア	Asia
オーストラリア	Australia
ヨーロッパ	Europe

にほん	Japan
ニュー・ジーランド	New Zealand
（きた）アメリカ	(North) America
（みなみ）アメリカ	(South) America

☺☺☺にすんでいます。	I/He/She/They live in ☺☺☺.

Look at the pictures of these children and write a sentence underneath each one describing where they live. Use one box for each letter and don't leave spaces between words. It's okay to move straight on to a new line even if you are in the middle of a word.

Which questions would you ask to get these answers? Use the vocabulary boxes at the tops of the previous pages to help you work it out!

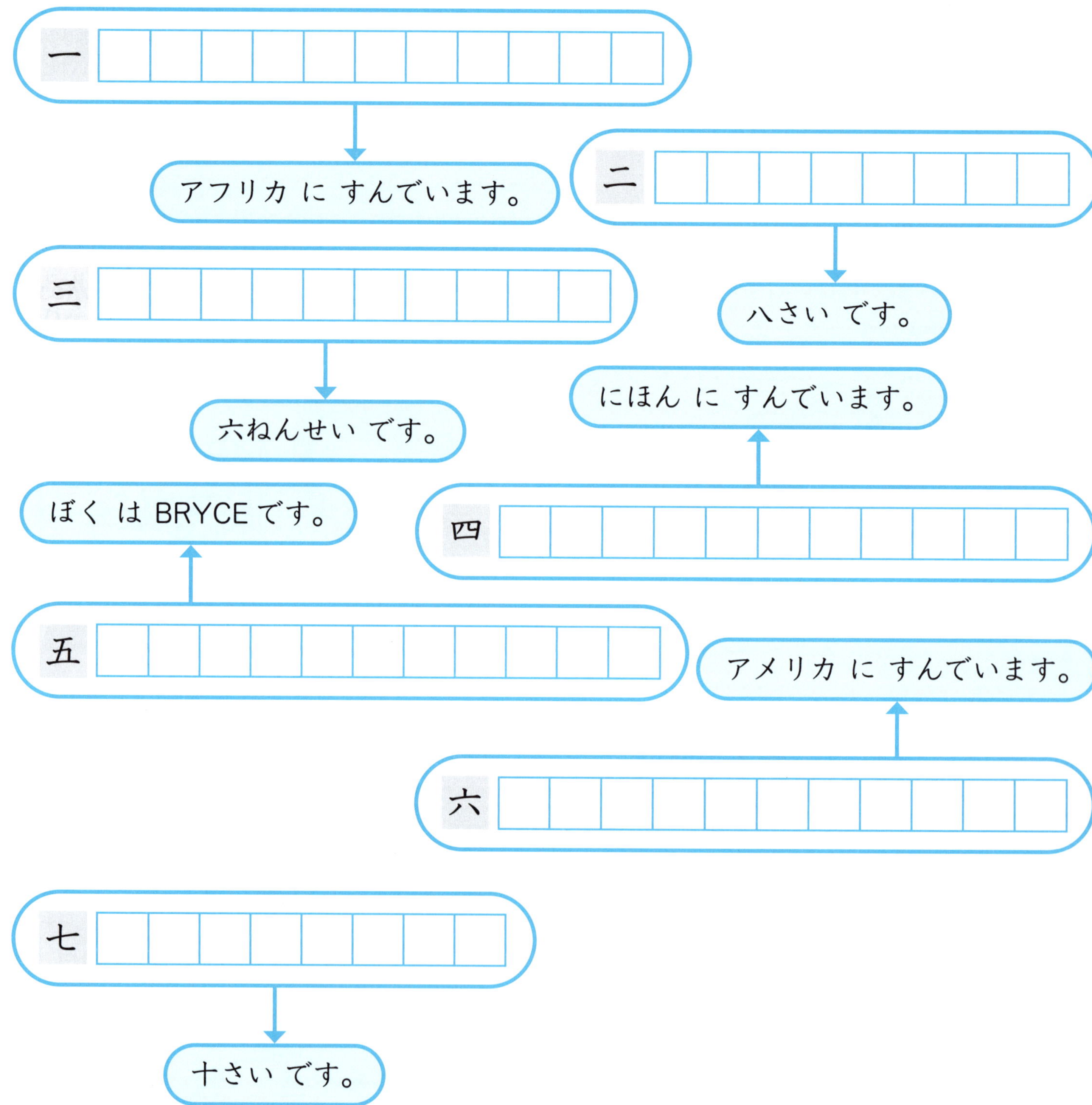

Fill in the numbers from 11 – 50 using kanji. Some of them have been done for you to trace over. Kanji are Chinese characters and they are usually a little more complicated than hiragana letters.

1	一
2	二
3	三
4	四
5	五
6	六
7	七
8	八
9	九
10	十

11		
12		
13	十	
14		四
15		
16		
17		
18		
19		
20	二	

21		十	
22			
23			
24			
25			
26			
27			七
28			
29			
30			

31			
32			
33	三	十	
34			
35			
36			六
37			
38			
39			
40			

41			
42			
43			
44	四	十	
45			
46			
47			
48			
49			
50			

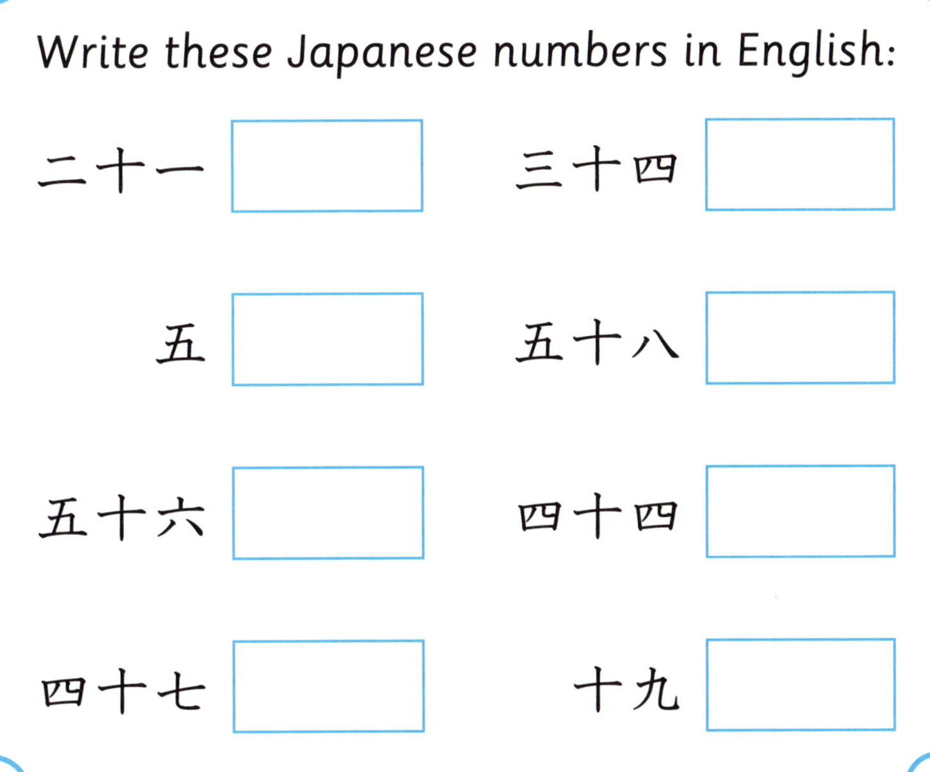

Discover the secret messages using the following code breaker:

a	1	e	5	i	9	m	13	q	17	u	21	y	25
b	2	f	6	j	10	n	14	r	18	v	22	z	26
c	3	g	7	k	11	o	15	s	19	w	23		
d	4	h	8	l	12	p	16	t	20	x	24		

Here are your secret messages. Be careful! You will have to change the numbers from Japanese to English to use the code breaker above.

二十三 ・ 五 ・ 十二 ・ 十二 ・ 四 ・ 十五 ・ 十四 ・ 五

1. What is the secret message? ______________________________

二十五 ・ 十五 ・ 二十一 ・ 一 ・ 十八 ・ 五 ・ 三 ・ 十二 ・ 五 ・ 二十二 ・ 五 ・ 十八

2. What is the secret message? ______________________________

五 ・ 一 ・ 十九 ・ 二十五 ・ 十六 ・ 五 ・ 一 ・ 十九 ・ 二十五 ・ 十 ・ 一 ・ 十六 ・ 一 ・ 十四 ・ 五 ・ 十九 ・ 二十五

3. What is the secret message? ______________________________

二十五 ・ 十五 ・ 二十一 ・ 一 ・ 十八 ・ 五 ・ 一 ・ 七 ・ 五 ・ 十四 ・ 九 ・ 二十一 ・ 十九

4. What is the secret message? ______________________________

十 ・ 一 ・ 十六 ・ 一 ・ 十四 ・ 五 ・ 十九 ・ 五 ・ 九 ・ 十九 ・ 三 ・ 十五 ・ 十五 ・ 十二

5. What is the secret message? ______________________________

Fill in the numbers from 51 – 100 using kanji.

51			
52			
53			
54			
55			
56			
57			
58			
59			
60			

61			
62			
63			
64			
65			
66			
67			
68			
69			
70			

71			
72			
73			
74			
75			
76			
77			
78			
79			
80			

81			
82			
83			
84			
85			
86			
87			
88			
89			
90			

91			
92			
93			
94			
95			
96			
97			
98			
99			
100	百		

Write these Japanese numbers in English:

九十二		八十四	
五十八		九十一	
七十四		八十三	
六十五		百	

EXTENSION LESSON 6 NUMBERS 51 – 100

Complete the dot-to-dot puzzle. Start at 五十 and count by 2's!

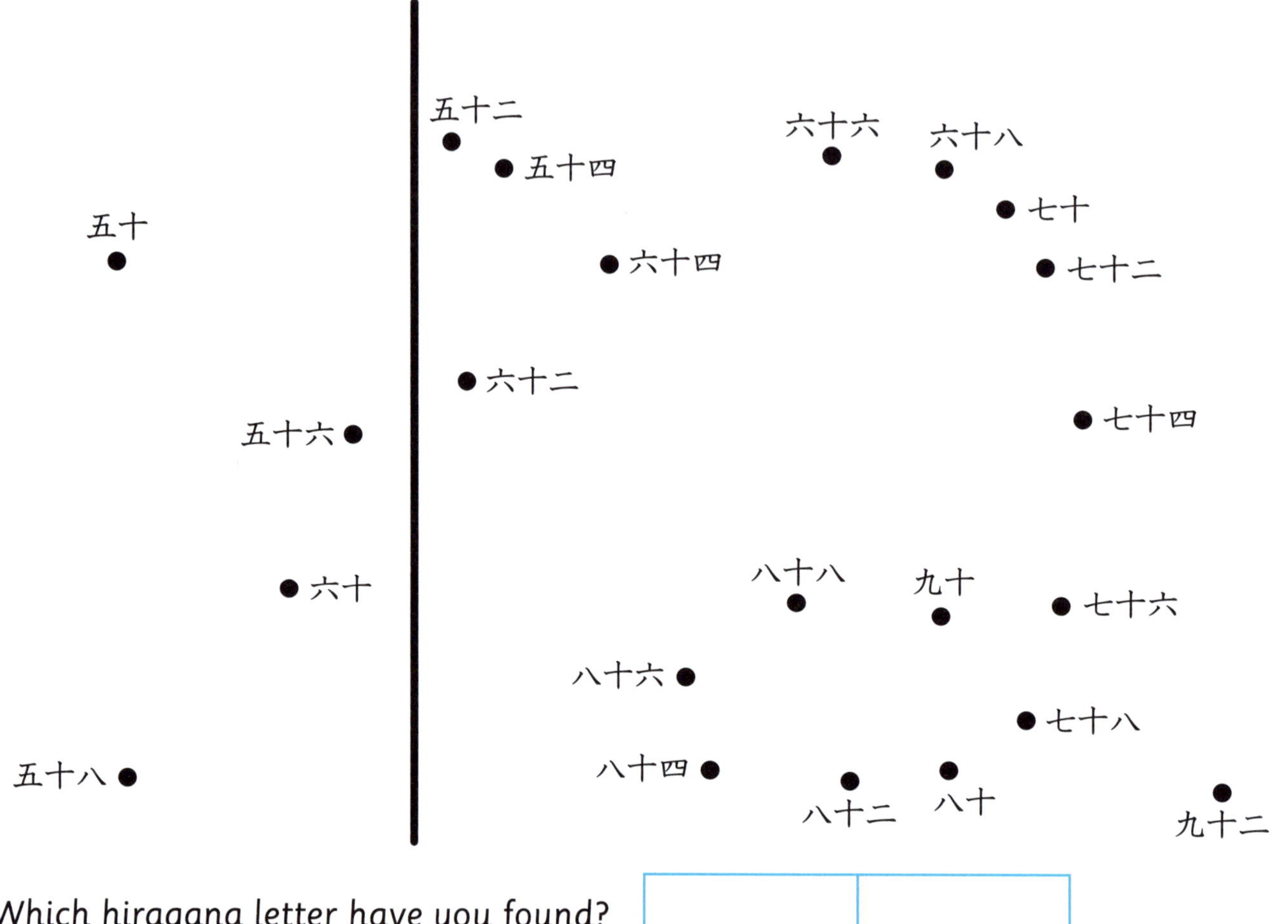

Which hiragana letter have you found?

HIRAGANA	ROMAJI

Use the square below to make your own hiragana dot-to-dot puzzle, then give it to a friend to try. Make sure you use Japanese numbers!

きいて ください。	Please listen.
みて ください。	Please look.
たって ください。	Please stand.
すわって ください。	Please sit.
しずか に して ください。	Please be quiet.
ほん を ひらいて ください。	Please open your book.
ほん を とじて ください。	Please close your book.

Trace over the hiragana letters, then fill in the blank boxes. Translate your sentence into English.

み		く	だ		い	。

English: ______________________________

ほ	ん		ひ	ら		て	く	だ		い	。

English: ______________________________

	ず		に		て		だ	さ		。

English: ______________________________

	ん		と		て			さ	い	。

English: ______________________________

す		っ	て				い	。

English: ______________________________

	い	て				い	

English: ______________________________

	っ		く				。

English: ______________________________

きいて ください。	Please listen.
みて ください。	Please look.
たって ください。	Please stand.
すわって ください。	Please sit.
しずか に して ください。	Please be quiet.
ほん を ひらいて ください。	Please open your book.
ほん を とじて ください。	Please close your book.

Only use the boxes you need!

What might your teacher say to you when:

she wants to explain something to you?

the class is very noisy?

he wants you to look at the television?

she wants you to begin your work?

he wants you to pack up?

you are out of your seat?

she wants you to stand up?

Can you remember your hiragana letter stroke order? Trace over the first stroke in red, the second in blue, and the third in yellow. If you can't remember, check the chart at the back of the book. Write the matching romaji underneath each box.

せ	も	か	ぬ	あ	お	わ	ゆ	み	わ

いちがつ	January	ごがつ	May	くがつ	September
にがつ	February	ろくがつ	June	じゅうがつ	October
さんがつ	March	しちがつ	July	じゅういちがつ	November
しがつ	April	はちがつ	August	じゅうにがつ	December

おたんじょうび は なんがつ です か。	What month is your birthday?
たんじょうび は ☺☺☺ がつ です。	My birthday is in ☺☺☺ (month).

Look at the months of the year and see if you can work out how they were named. There is another way to write the months, using kanji numbers. Trace over the examples, then complete the grid.

いちがつ	一がつ	January	しちがつ		July
にがつ	二がつ	February	はちがつ		August
さんがつ	三がつ	March	くがつ		September
しがつ		April	じゅうがつ		October
ごがつ		May	じゅういちがつ		November
ろくがつ		June	じゅうにがつ		December

Find five people in the class and ask them:

おたんじょうび は なんがつ です か。 → What month is your birthday?

Your partner should answer:

☺☺☺ がつ です。 → ☺☺☺ (month).

Record the answers to your question below.

Student's name	Birthday month in Japanese	Birthday month in English

Max is going on a school excursion to Japan during the holidays. When he arrives at Narita Airport, near Tokyo, he must answer the immigration official's questions. Look at Max's passport to get the information you need to help Max answer the official's questions properly. Write Max's answers in his speech bubbles. Consult the vocabulary boxes from previous lessons if you need help.

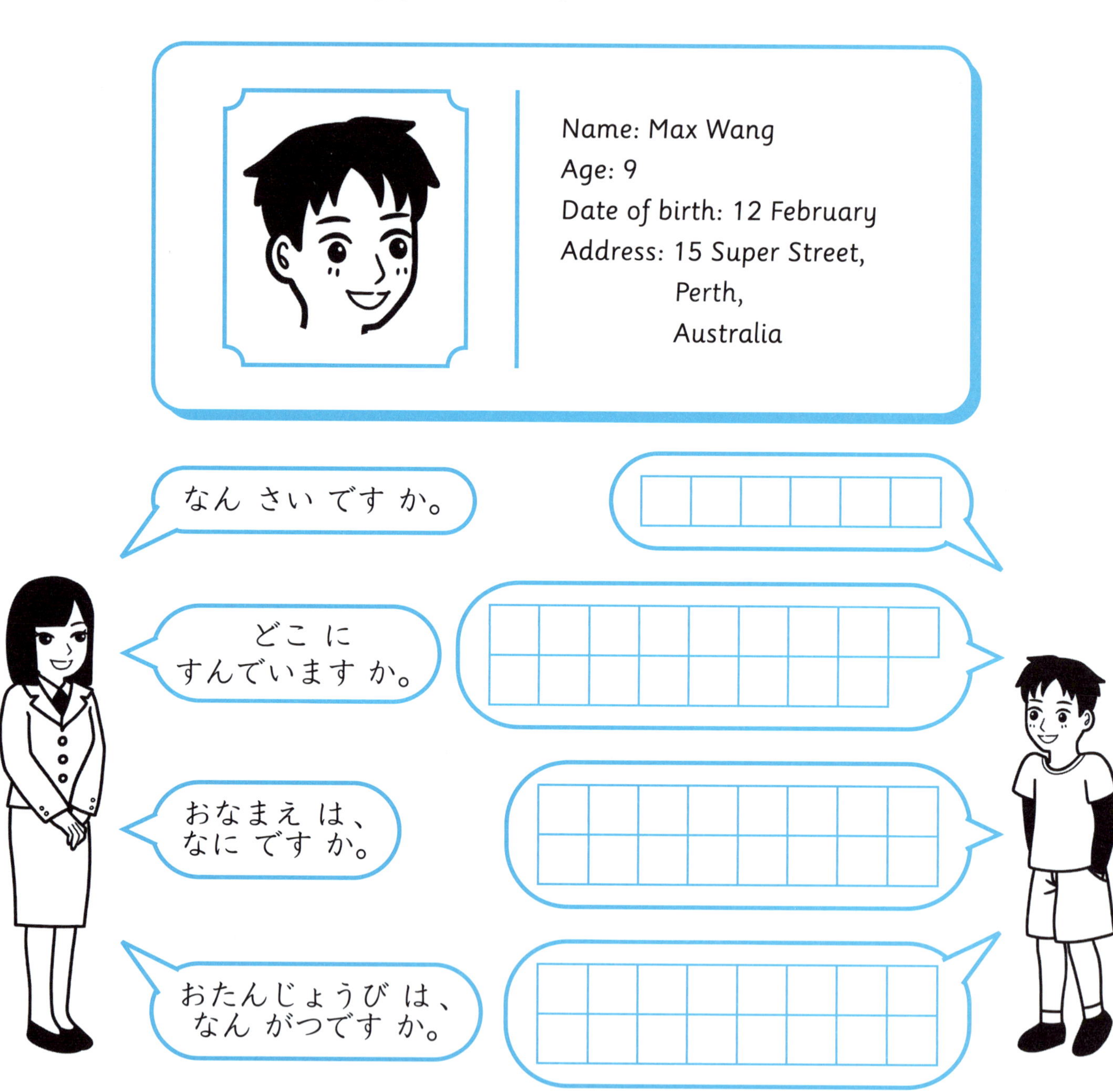

Fill in the matching Japanese word.

March		your birthday		August	
February		November		June	
December		my birthday		July	

なつ	summer
あき	autumn

ふゆ	winter
はる	spring

☺☺☺がすきです。	I like ☺☺☺.

Trace over the Japanese words, then match the activity with the season by joining them with a line.

あき	swimming
はる	skiing
なつ	raking leaves
ふゆ	picking flowers

Write a sentence in Japanese saying which season each child likes. The first sentence has been done for you to trace over, as an example.

Look at the words you have learned so far to answer these questions in Japanese.

一 The coldest season of the year:

二 The month of your birth:

三 The largest island of Japan:

四 The number after 六十八:

五 The continent closest to みなみ アメリカ:

六 The season before ふゆ:

七 The month before January:

八 The northernmost island of Japan:

九 New Zealand's closest large neighbour:

十 The hottest season of the year:

十一 The opposite season to あき:

十二 The number that is half of 八十六:

十三 The Japanese word meaning 'please':

十四 The Japanese word meaning 'what':

十五 The Japanese word meaning 'where':

十六 The capital city of Japan:

十七 The number that is twice 五十:

Translate the clues to discover the hidden word in the shaded boxes. Write your answers using hiragana letters.

How old are you? 。

August (use hiragana)

I like … … 。

summer

The hidden word was:

Japanese	English

なつ	summer
あき	autumn
ふゆ	winter
はる	spring

は

particle WA

あつい	hot
すずしい	cool
さむい	cold
あたたかい	warm

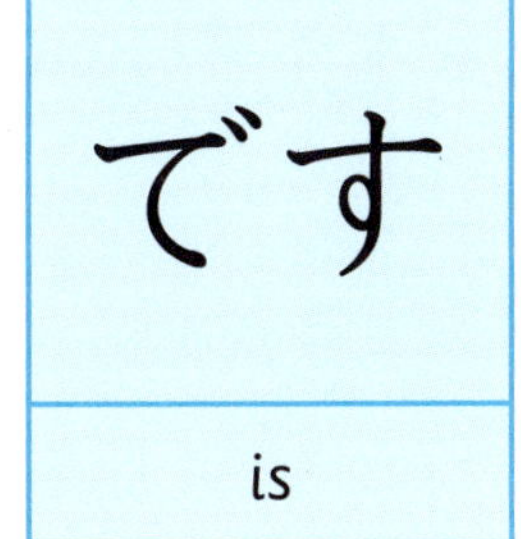

is

☺A☺ は、 ☺B☺ です。	☺A☺ is ☺B☺ .

Trace over the season words in 

and the temperature words in 

.

The Weather Song

(to the tune of Scarborough Fair)

なつ は、 あつい です。

あき は、 すずしい です。

ふゆ は、 さむい です。

はる は、 あたたかい です。

Circle the mistake in each scenario, then rewrite the sentence correctly. The first one has been done for you to trace over.

一 なつ は、(さむい) です。 なつ は、 あつい です。

二 あき、すずしい です。 ______

三 あき は、すずし です。 ______

四 なつ は、あすい です。 ______

五 ふゆ は、あつい です。 ______

六 ふゆ は、きむい です。 ______

七 なし は、あつい です。 ______

八 はる は、あたたかい どす。 ______

なつ	summer
あき	autumn
ふゆ	winter
はる	spring

particle WA

あつい	hot
すずしい	cool
さむい	cold
あたたかい	warm

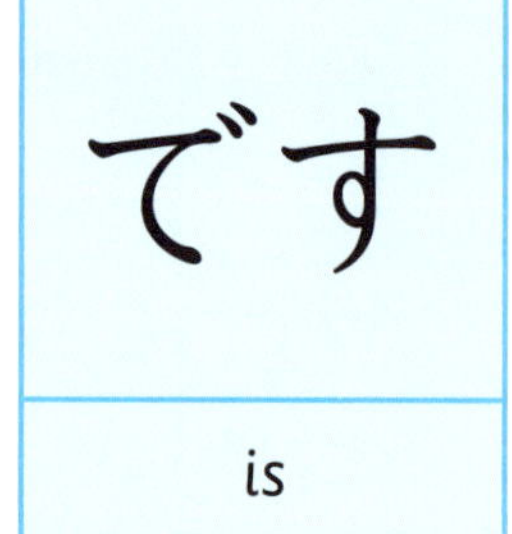

is

Collect the hiragana letters along the correct path to make the mystery sentence.

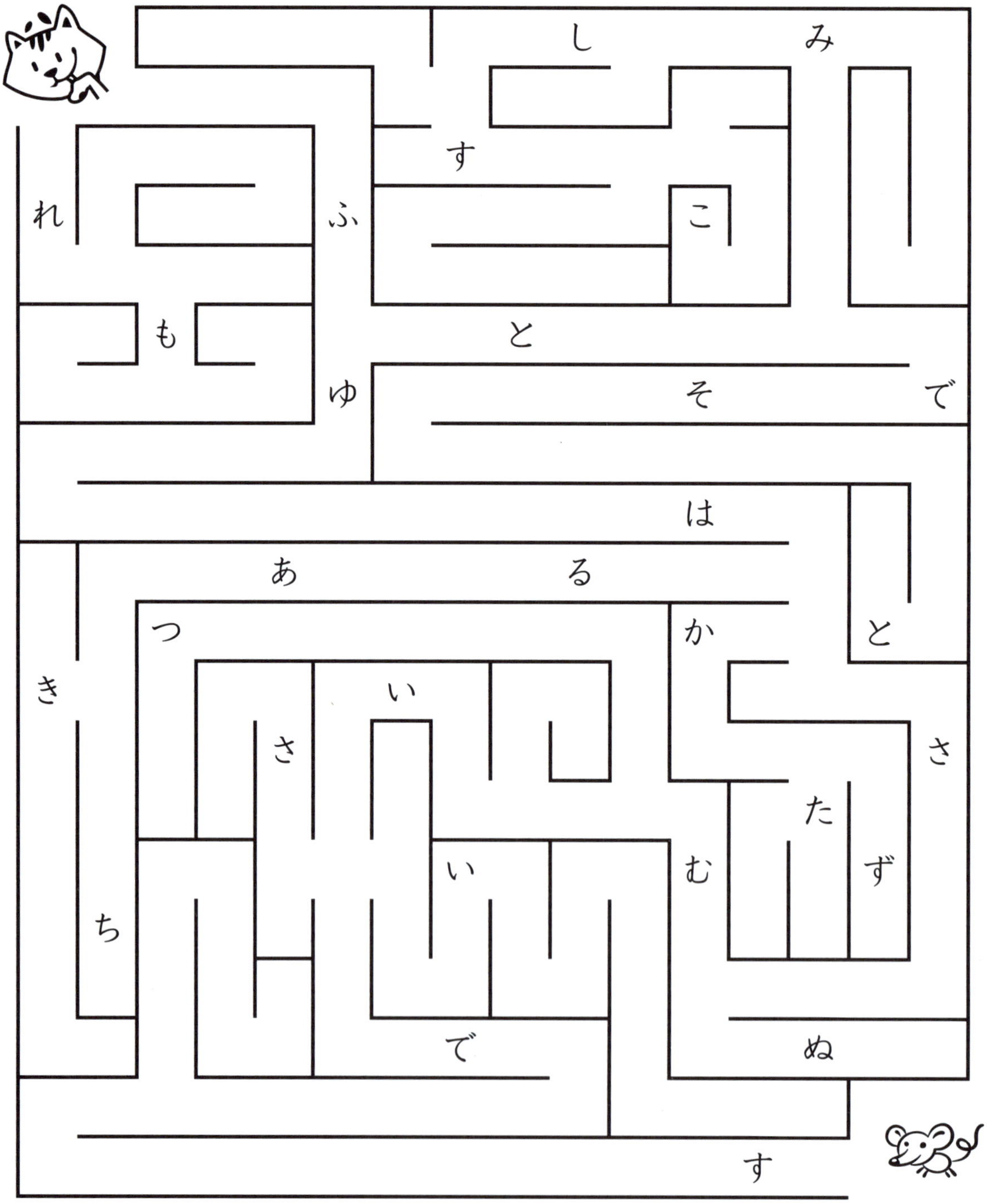

し み
す
れ ふ こ
も と
ゆ そ で
は
あ る
つ か と
き い
さ さ
た
い む ず
ち
で ぬ
す

Japanese:				、						。
English:										

なつ	summer
あき	autumn
ふゆ	winter
はる	spring

は
particle WA

あつい	hot
すずしい	cool
さむい	cold
あたたかい	warm

です
is

か
question particle

Look at these two sentences:

なつ は、あつい です。→ Summer is hot.

なつ は、あつい です か。→ Is summer hot?

What happened to the second Japanese sentence to make it into a question?

____

Change the following sentences into questions, then translate them into English. The first one has been done for you to trace over.

		STATEMENT	QUESTION
JAPANESE:	一	あき は、すずしい です。	あき は、すずしい です か。
ENGLISH:	1	Autumn is cool.	Is autumn cool?
JAPANESE:	二	ふゆ は、あたたかい です。	
ENGLISH:	2		
JAPANESE:	三	なつ は、さむい です。	
ENGLISH:	3		
JAPANESE:	四	ふゆ は、あつい です。	
ENGLISH:	4		
JAPANESE:	五	はる は、あたたかい です。	
ENGLISH:	5		
JAPANESE:	六	なつ は、すずしい です。	
ENGLISH:	6		

Use the information from earlier lessons to help you complete the crossword. Translate (or complete) the clues to solve the puzzle. Write your answers using hiragana letters, not kanji!

	1.	2.		3.						4.			5.
												6.	
	7.		8.			9.							
					10.							11.	
				12.				13.	14.				
			15.				16.				17.		
18.										19.			
	20.				21.								22.
23.				24.		25.				26.			
	27.							28.					

Clues down

2. book
3. Japan
4. cool
5. listen
7. your name
8. what
9. spring
11. this year
12. north
14. this (Language Lesson 16)
15. hot
16. January
18. はる ____ すき です。
19. どうぞ ____ 。
21. one (1)
22. summer
25. month

Clues across

1. I live in Japan.
6. yes (Language Lesson 12)
8. what
9. I'm pleased to meet you.
10. spring
13. where
15. warm
17. and also
20. cold
23. なん さい です ____ 。
24. August
26. July
27. south
28. おなまえ ____、なん です か。

Use the vocabulary boxes from the previous lessons, and the words below, to help you complete the question-and-answer activities.

Answer these questions about Japan with  はい or いいえ.

1. Do Japanese people wash in the bath? __________
2. Is Osaka the capital city of Japan? __________
3. Do Japanese people drink tea? __________
4. Is potato the most commonly eaten food in Japan? __________
5. Do Japanese people take off their shoes before entering their houses? __________
6. Is the traditional dress of Japan called the kimono? __________
7. Do they use chopsticks in Japan? __________
8. Is French the national language of Japan? __________

Answer the following Japanese questions with はい or いいえ.
The first one has been done for you to trace over.

一 なつ は、あついですか。 はい

二 にほん に すんでいます か。 __________

三 六ねんせい です か。 __________

四 八がつ は、なつ です か。 __________

五 なつ が すき です か。 __________

Use the vocabulary boxes from the previous lessons to help you complete the question-and-answer activities.

Trace over the hiragana letters, then fill in the missing 'yes' or 'no' words to complete the question-and-answer pairs.

一	Q:	あきがすきですか。
	A:	＿＿＿＿、あきがすきです。
二	Q:	なつは、あついですか。
	A:	＿＿＿＿、なつは、あついです。
三	Q:	三ねんせいですか。
	A:	＿＿＿＿、四ねんせいです。
四	Q:	ふゆは、あついですか。
	A:	＿＿＿＿、ふゆは、あついです。

はい

いいえ

Follow the lines to find out where each of these children lives, then answer はい or いいえ to the questions below.

一 SAM くん は、アメリカ に すんでいます か。 ＿＿＿＿

二 ANTONIA さん は、ニュー・ジーランド に すんでいます か。 ＿＿＿＿

三 DEREK くん は、ヨーロッパ に すんでいます か。 ＿＿＿＿

四 MELISSA さん は、オーストラリア に すんでいます か。 ＿＿＿＿

五 DEREK くん は、ニュー・ジーランド に すんでいます か。 ＿＿＿＿

六 SAM くん は、ヨーロッパ に すんでいます か。 ＿＿＿＿

ホットドッグ	hot dog
サンドイッチ	sandwich
ピザ	pizza
ハンバーガー	hamburger
やきそば	fried noodles

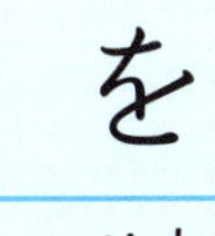

particle O

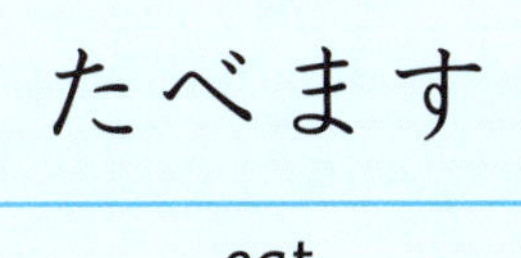

eat

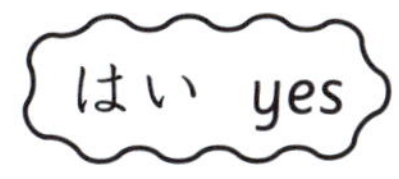

☺☺☺ を たべます。	I will eat ☺☺☺. (I would like ☺☺☺.)
なに を たべます か。	What will you eat? (What would you like to eat?)
☺☺☺ を たべます か。	Will you eat ☺☺☺? (Would you like ☺☺☺?)

Trace over the dialogue, then answer the questions below using 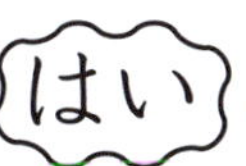 はい or いいえ.

1. Will Erin eat a hamburger?	
2. Will Ben eat a hot dog?	
3. Will Tahlia eat a pizza?	
4. Will Mike eat a sandwich?	
5. Will Mike eat a pizza?	

Fill in the matching Japanese words:	
1. eat	
2. what	
3. fried noodles	
4. question particle	

Trace over the questions below, then answer in Japanese using the pictures as a guide. Use the vocabulary boxes from previous lessons to help you.

一 なに を たべます か。

二 ピザ を たべます か。

三 やきそば が すき です か。

四 サンドイッチ が すき です か。

五 ホットドッグ を たべます か。

Can you remember your hiragana letter stroke order? For each hiragana letter, trace over the first stroke in red, the second in blue, and the third in yellow. If you can't remember, check the chart at the back of the book. Write the matching romaji underneath each box.

な	も	け	に	あ	き	わ	ぬ	と	む

か	ね	す	は	ま	た	ほ	せ	ふ	ち

みず	water
ジュース	juice
ミルク	milk
おちゃ	green tea
コーヒー	coffee

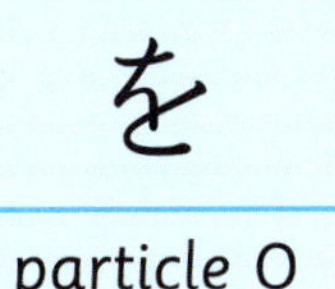

particle O

のみます
drink

☺☺☺ を のみます。	I will drink ☺☺☺. (I would like ☺☺☺.)
なに を のみます か。	What will you drink ? (What would you like to drink?)
☺☺☺ を のみます か。	Will you drink ☺☺☺? (Would you like ☺☺☺?)

What might you say in Japanese in the following situations? Use as many boxes as you need and don't forget the full stop!

一 You are working in a fast food store when a Japanese man comes in. He looks very tired and thirsty.

二 A small child approaches you and says she is thirsty. You offer her a glass of milk.

三 You go into a restaurant and would like to order a glass of juice.

四 You are asked if you would like a soft drink but you would prefer a glass of water.

五 You bring your father a cup of coffee and ask him if he would like it.

Trace over the words written correctly, then write their meanings in English underneath. Put a cross through any words written incorrectly.

みつ

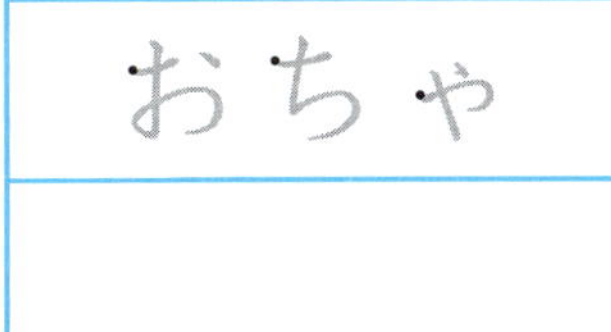

コーフー

Using the vocabulary boxes from previous lessons, unjumble the words to make a question. Write the question in the boxes provided and give an appropriate answer underneath. Use as many boxes as you need, but don't leave spaces between words!

一 のみます　おちゃ　を　か　。

Q:

A:

二 。　を　たべます　ピザ　か。

Q:

A:

三 か　なに　。　のみます　を

Q:

A:

四 は　なん　か　おなまえ　。　です

Q:

A:

五 ミルク　のみます　か　を　。

Q:

A:

六 に　すんでいます　か　。　どこ

Q:

A:

七 。　さい　なん　か　です

Q:

A:

いただきます。	always said before eating
すみません。	Excuse me.
☺☺☺ を ください。	May I have ☺☺☺ ?
どうぞ。	Here you are. OR Go ahead. (Please eat.)
ごちそうさまでした。	Thank you for the food.

Read about Jess' first time in a Japanese restaurant. As you go along, fill in the blank boxes with the appropriate Japanese word.

It was almost time to go to the restaurant! Jess had only been in Tokyo for one week and she was really looking forward to going to her first sushi restaurant. Jess did not really know what sushi was but her Japanese host family had told her that it was one of the most famous dishes in Japan, so she was very keen to try it. At the restaurant, Jess and her host family sat around a revolving counter, where small dishes full of exotic looking raw fish on little rice balls slowly passed them by. The children were allowed to choose whatever they liked and they soon started taking dishes from the counter. Jess took a beautiful gold dish with two small pieces of sushi on it. She was just about to put the sushi in her mouth when her host mother and sisters all looked at her disapprovingly. Oh no, what had she done wrong? Then she noticed each of her host sisters say, ______ . Oh, she had forgotten her Japanese manners!

Jess also said, ______ and then popped one of her sushi pieces in her mouth. Mmmm! Jess thought it was quite tasty. But suddenly, she had the most terrible feeling inside her nose, just as if there were a bomb exploding in there. She pointed frantically at the water and said, ______ , みず______ . Her host family were laughing so much, they almost forgot to pass the water. They knew that the reason Jess was gasping for water was that she had chosen some sushi with lots of wasabi on it. Wasabi is the green spicy paste that is hidden under the layer of fish on the top of the small rice ball. Jess found out what happens when you eat a piece of sushi with too much wasabi on it!

______ , said her host mother as she passed the water, and wiped away her tears of laughter. Surprisingly, Jess enjoyed the exploding sensation of the wasabi and, after two or three more pieces, she began to think that sushi was the most delicious thing that she had ever eaten. When everyone was full to bursting, the waitress came and counted the number of plates that they had taken from the revolving counter and added up the bill. Jess was determined not to forget her manners again, so before anyone reminded her she said gratefully, ______ !

Can you remember these words? Try and write the missing Japanese or English words without looking them up. If you need to, check previous vocabulary boxes for help.

	I'm pleased to meet you.
たべます	
	where
いいえ	
ピザ	
	Japan
	37
	March
八がつ	

おちゃ	
	what
	64
のみます	
	warm
あれ	
	please
すわって	
	autumn

	summer
これ	
七十五	
	December
四がつ	
	cold
しずか	
	yes
あつい	

Using the vocabulary boxes from previous lessons, make up your own dialogue between yourself and a Japanese friend. Imagine that you have invited this friend to dinner at your house, and you are sitting at the table ready to eat. Use as many boxes as you wish to write a short dialogue that might take place at the dinner table.

You:															
Your friend:															
You:															
Your friend:															
You:															
Your friend:															
You:															
Your friend:															
You:															
Your friend:															

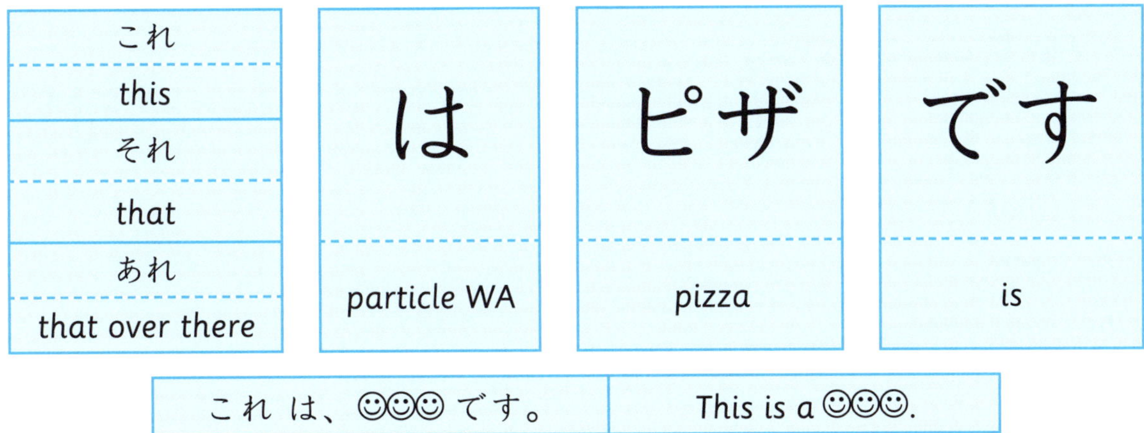

Label each animal's favourite foods with 'this' これ, 'that' それ, or 'that over there' あれ. The first one has been done for you to trace over.

Each person in the cartoon would like to tell us that the food on the table is a pizza. Trace over the letters and fill in the missing word(s) in each speech bubble so that they all have a turn. Make sure you use これ, それ or あれ in your sentence.

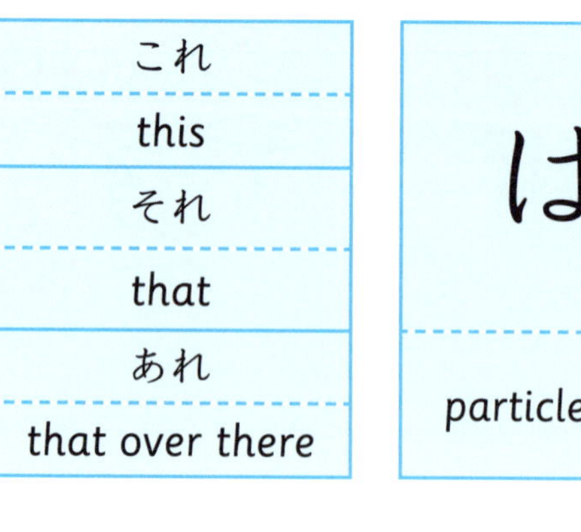

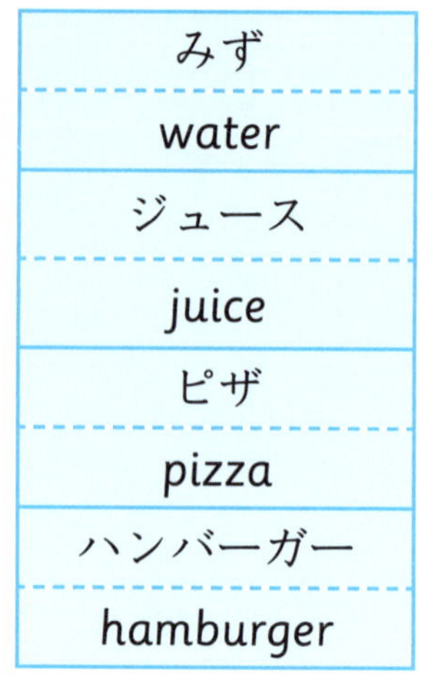

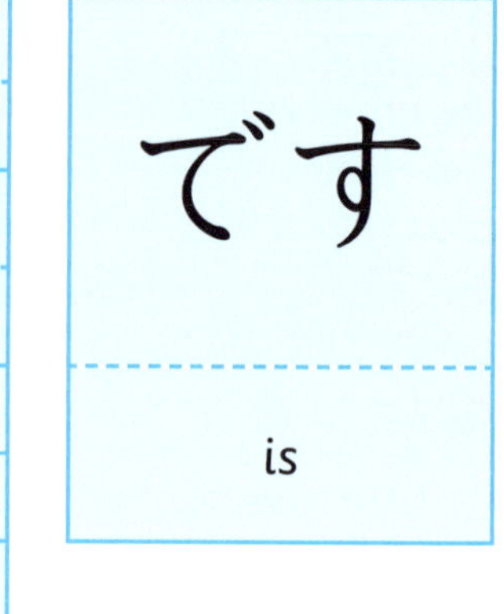

Follow the lines to make each sentence, then rewrite them in the boxes below. Draw a picture to show what each sentence means.

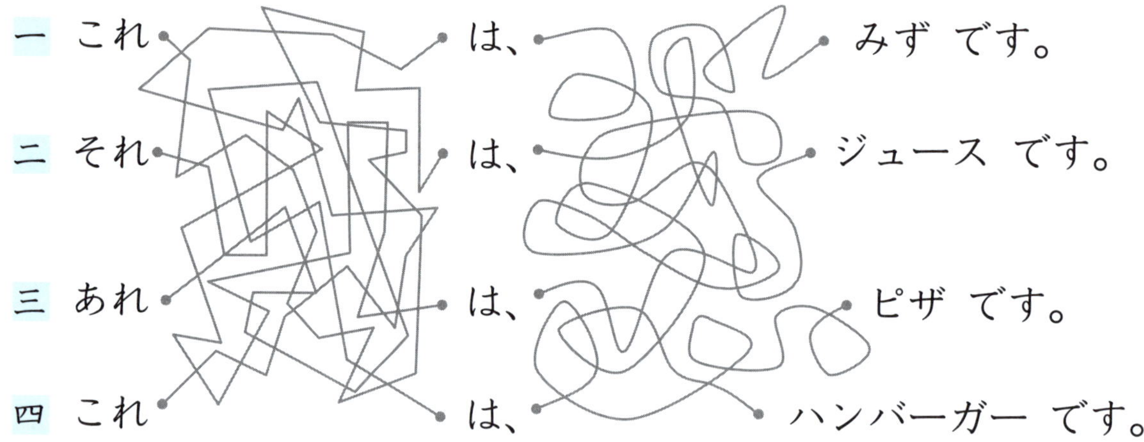

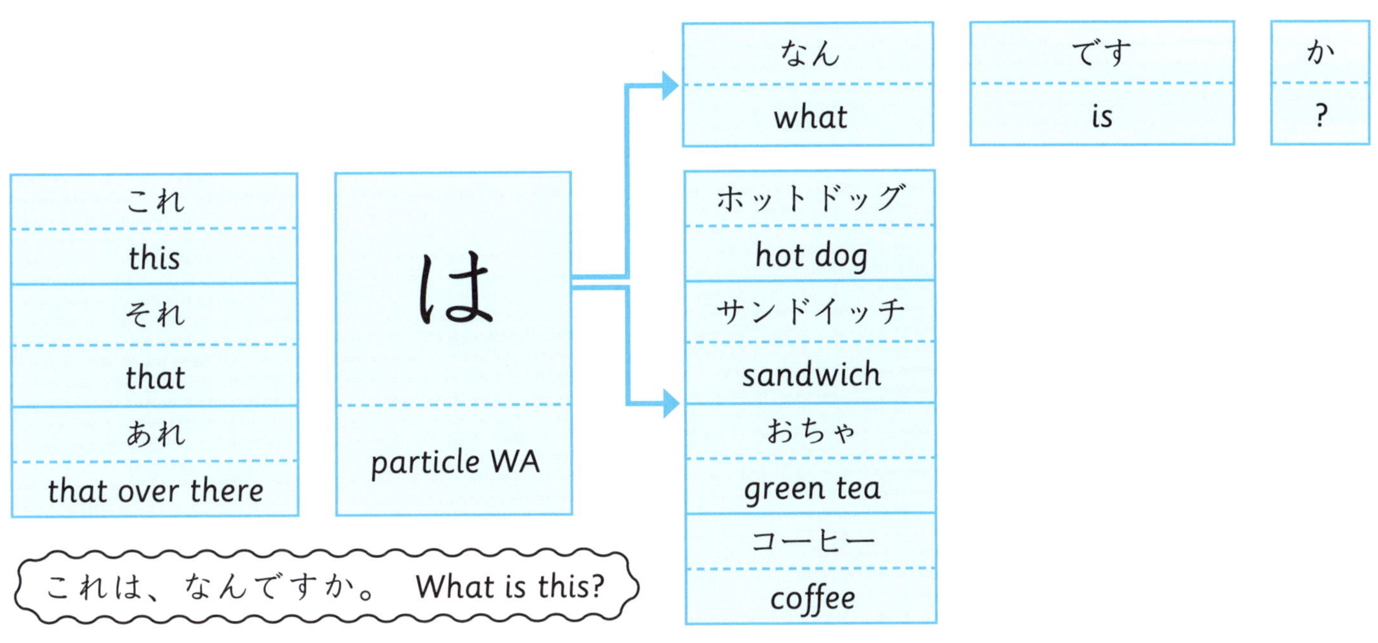

Trace over the Japanese sentences in the speech bubbles, then choose the correct sentence for each empty speech bubble from the box below and write it in.

これ は、なん です か。 それ は、サンドイッチ です。
あれ は、ホットドッグ です。 あれ は、なん です か。

あれ は、なん です か。

それ は、おちゃ です。

これ は、なん です か。

あれ は、コーヒー です。

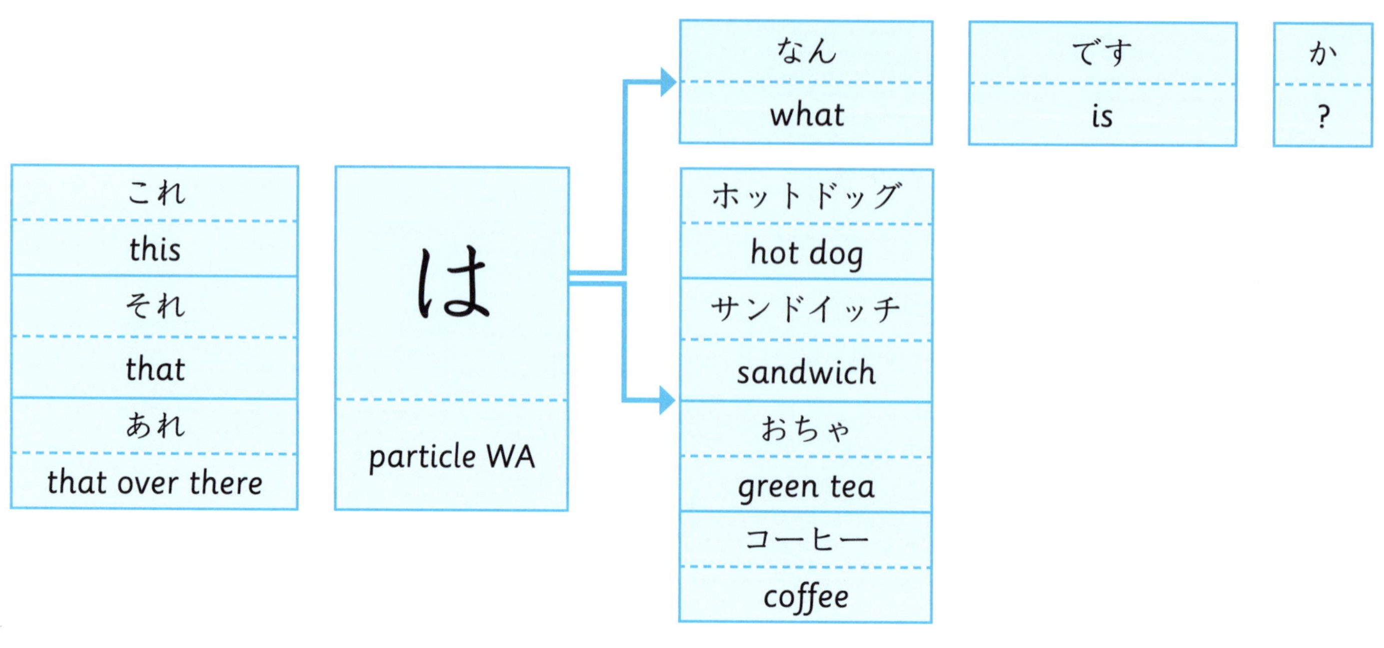

Translate each sentence into Japanese, then follow the instructions below.

一 What is that over there?

			、						。

二 That over there is a hot dog.

			、									。

Now follow (in the correct order) each letter in sentence one, then sentence two, to lead you to the name of the samurai. The samurai's name is: □□□□

がっこう	school
こうえん	park
みせ	shop(s)

えいがかん	cinema
どうぶつえん	zoo
うみ	sea/beach

これ は、☺☺☺ です。	This is ☺☺☺.

Complete the unfinished pictures, then label your drawings with an appropriate sentence. The first one has been done for you to trace over. Use as many boxes as you need.

Using the vocabulary boxes from the previous lessons, find and trace over as many complete sentences as you can find in the sentence search. Write five of your sentences in the boxes below the sentence search, with their meanings in English underneath.

さ	も	い	む	。	み	あ	か	ピ	ザ	を	た	べ	ま	す	。	に
が	っ	こ	う	に	い	き	ま	す	。	た	な	と	に	け	こ	ゆ
に	せ	あ	な	つ	と	は	ぬ	ら	よ	そ	い	ま	ほ	の	く	お
こ	と	て	な	つ	が	す	き	で	す	。	し	み	ん	え	ら	。
わ	。	ひ	そ	よ	。	ず	た	め	さ	ち	と	こ	に	む	く	け
し	は	。	ね	あ	ら	し	り	て	。	む	さ	う	す	け	て	ぬ
は	を	の	ん	。	や	い	る	い	え	か	。	り	ん	き	み	き
こ	れ	は	お	ち	ゃ	で	す	。	は	っ	さ	い	で	す	。	つ
も	や	う	つ	も	を	す	ふ	そ	。	ふ	お	へ	い	ち	ま	く
え	す	せ	し	め	ん	。	へ	に	か	き	れ	ろ	ま	ほ	ぬ	わ
う	た	ん	じ	ょ	う	び	は	は	ち	が	つ	で	す	。	ま	か
ひ	あ	。	の	。	ね	ゆ	る	。	よ	み	ろ	ほ	。	な	め	そ

Japanese:	
English:	
Japanese:	
English:	
Japanese:	
English:	
Japanese:	
English:	
Japanese:	
English:	

がっこう	school		えいがかん	cinema
こうえん	park		どうぶつえん	zoo
みせ	shop(s)		うみ	sea/beach

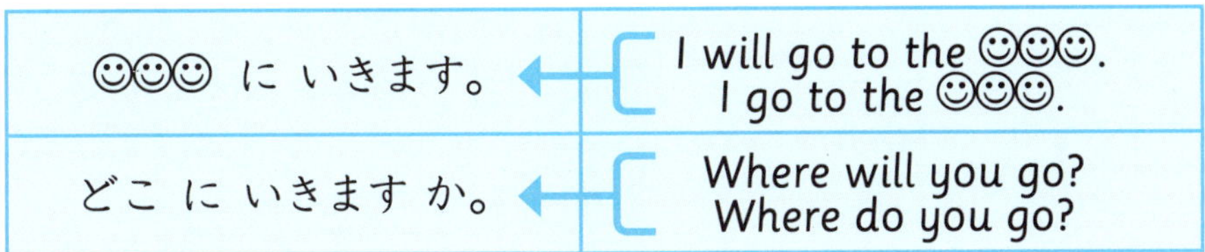

☺☺☺ に いきます。	I will go to the ☺☺☺. I go to the ☺☺☺.
どこ に いきます か。	Where will you go? Where do you go?

Hana is planning her calendar for next year. Every month she wants to go to a different place. Fill in her calendar for the first four months of the year, using her pictures as a guide. January has been done for you to trace over.

一がつ

どうぶつえんにいきます。

Read the information in the speech bubble and answer the questions underneath. Answer the English questions in English, and the Japanese questions in Japanese.

	せんせい	= teacher
	九じ	= 9 o'clock
	に	= to (a place)
also	に	= in (a season)
also	に	= at (a time)

はじめまして。
ぼく は、せんせい です。
なまえ は、さとう です。
にほん に すんでいます。
三十五さい です。
たんじょうび は、六がつ です。
はる が すき です。
はる に こうえん に いきます。
ピザ が すきです。ピザ を たべます。
みず を のみます。
九じ に がっこう に いきます。
どうぞ よろしく。

1 What is this man's job? __________

2 What is this man's name? __________

3 Where does he live? __________

4 How old is he? __________

5 What month is his birthday? __________

6 Where does he go in spring? __________

7 What does he like to eat? __________

8 When does he go to school? __________

一 さとう さん は、なん さい です か。

二 なに を たべます か。

三 ピザ が すき です か。

四 どこ に すんでいます か。

五 九じ に どこ に いきます か。

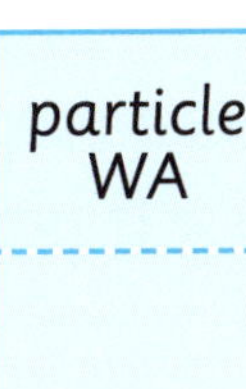
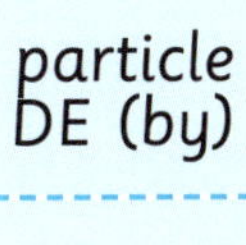

	particle WA		particle DE (by)		particle NI (to)	go
はな さん Hana - san	は	ひこうき plane	で	にほん Japan	に	いきます
Kara さん Kara - san		くるま car		がっこう school		
Bryce くん Bryce - kun		バス bus		どうぶつえん zoo		
たか くん Taka - kun		じてんしゃ bicycle		みせ shops		
		でんしゃ train				

Read the following information, then label the Japanese sentences with はい if they are true or いいえ if they are false.

Bryce's family doesn't have a car, so he always travels by bicycle. Kara is afraid of heights, so she can't travel by plane. Taka loves planes and goes to Japan every year on one. Hana goes to school by train but uses the bus when she goes to the zoo.

一 BRYCE くん は、くるま で がっこう に いきます。 ________

二 KARA さん は、ひこうき で にほん に いきます。 ________

三 たか くん は、ひこうき で にほん に いきます。 ________

四 はな さん は、でんしゃ で がっこう に いきます。 ________

五 はな さん は、でんしゃ で どうぶつえん に いきます。 ________

Add appropriate words to the following sentences, so that they make sense.

一 [ ] は、[ ] で がっこう に いきます。

二 たか くん は、ひこうき で [ ] に いきます。

三 KARA さん は、でんしゃ [ ] みせ に [ ] 。

四 [ ] くん は、[ ] で どうぶつえん に いきます。

JAPANESE CHALLENGE!! A Japanese person tells you they are going somewhere. You want to find out how they are getting there. What would you say? (Hint: なに= what)

Look at the bottom of p.44 for the correct answer.

Read the following passage, then answer the questions in Japanese using full sentences. Refer to the vocabulary boxes in previous lessons only if you have to.

MELISSA さん の = MELISSA's
に = in [a season]

MELISSA さん は、にほん に すんでいます。
はる に ひこうき で アフリカ に いきます。
アフリカ が すき です。
そして ふゆ に ひこうき で アメリカ に いきます。
MELISSA さん は、四ねんせい です。
がっこう が すき です。
MELISSA さん の たんじょうび は、十二がつ です。
十さい です。
たんじょうび に どうぶつえん に いきます。

一 MELISSA さん は、どこ に すんでいます か。

____

二 MELISSA さん は、なつ に アフリカ に いきます か。

____

三 MELISSA さん は、アフリカ が すき です か。

____

四 MELISSA さん は、くるま で アメリカ に いきます か。

____

五 MELISSA さん は、なん ねんせい です か。

____

六 MELISSA さん の たんじょうび は、なん がつ です か。

____

七 MELISSA さん は、なん さい です か。

____

八 MELISSA さん の たんじょうび に どこ に いきます か。

____

[To find out how someone is getting somewhere, you ask: By what will you go? – なに で いきます か。]

When you see a small っ, pause for a moment before continuing your word.

To write a small っ in romaji, use the first romaji letter that follows the small っ. This will make a double letter, like this:

Trace over the examples in the first row, then complete the chart yourself.

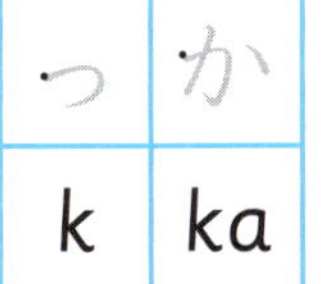
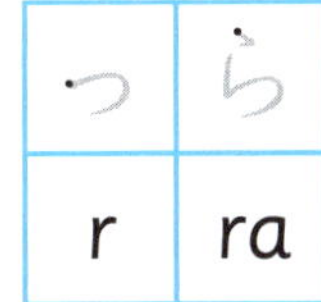
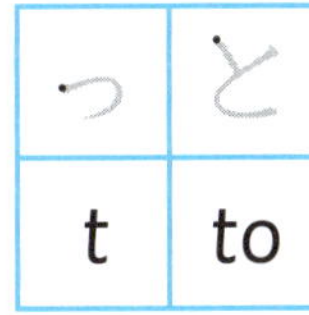
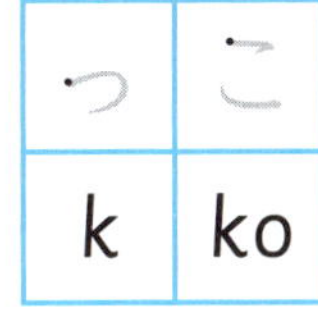
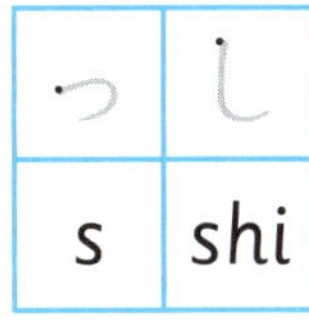

っ	か	っ	ら	っ	と	っ	こ	っ	し	っ	ぽ
k	ka	r	ra	t	to	k	ko	s	shi	p	po

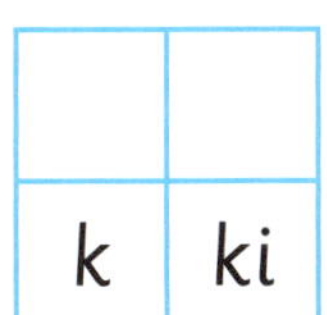
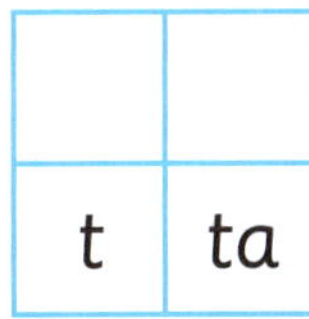
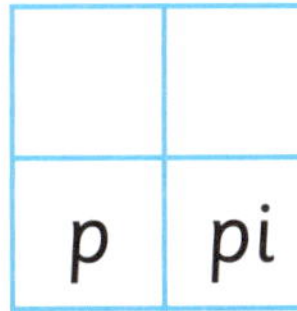
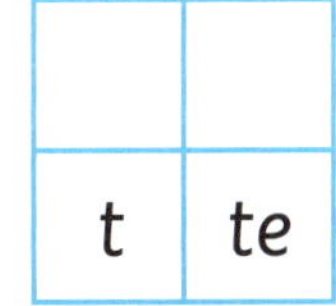

k	ki	t	ta	p	pi	k	ke	s	su	t	te

BEWARE! Small っ is never used before the 'm' and 'n' hiragana letters. Instead of small っ the hiragana letter ん is used, like this:

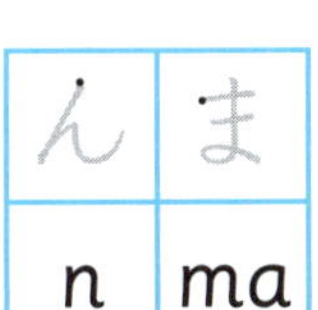
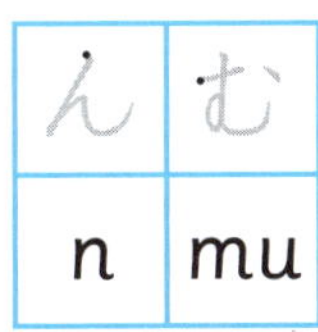
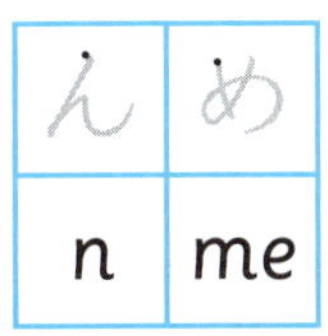

ん	ま	ん	み	ん	む	ん	め	ん	も
n	ma	n	mi	n	mu	n	me	n	mo

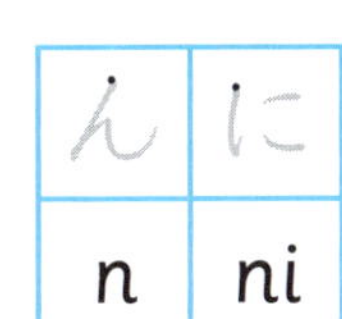
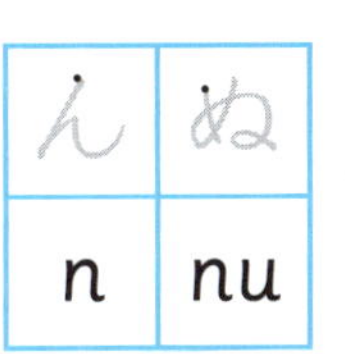
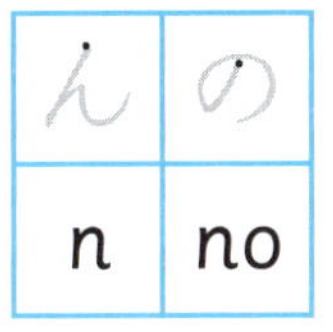

ん	な	ん	に	ん	ぬ	ん	ね	ん	の
n	na	n	ni	n	nu	n	ne	n	no

Trace over the examples.

Fill in the blank boxes with the missing hiragana or romaji letters.

は		さ	
	s		i

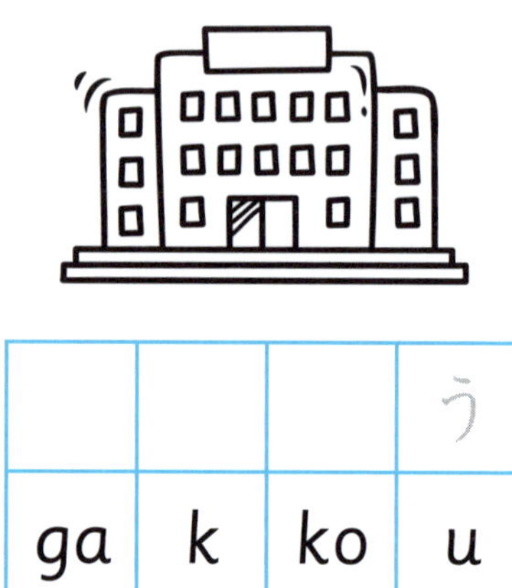

			う
ga	k	ko	u

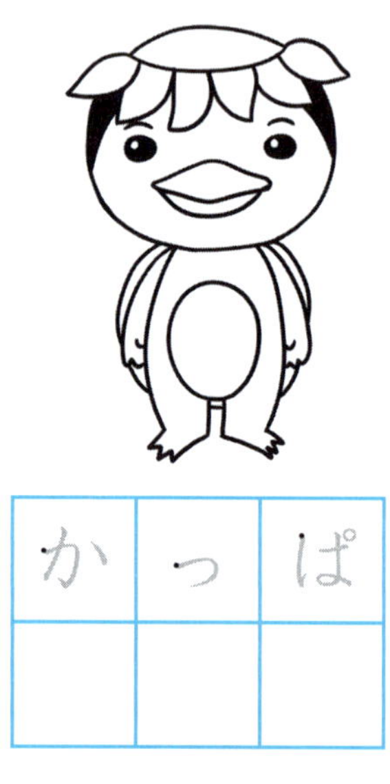

か	っ	ぱ

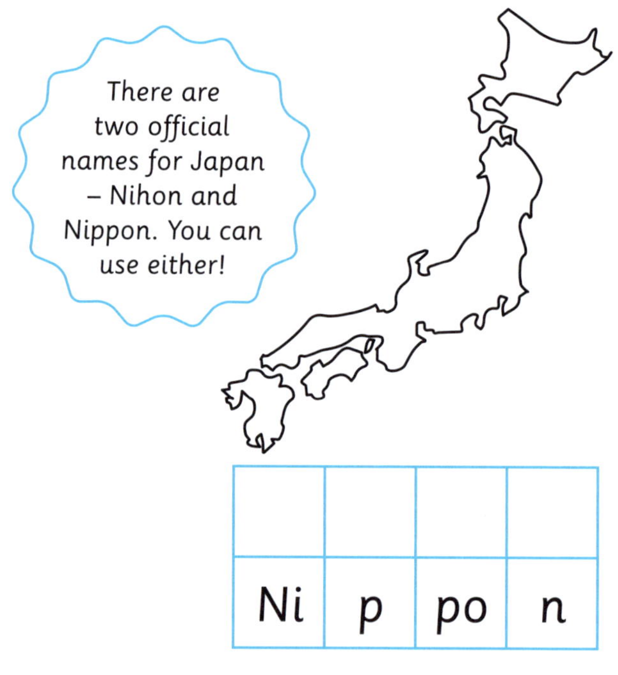

Ni	p	po	n

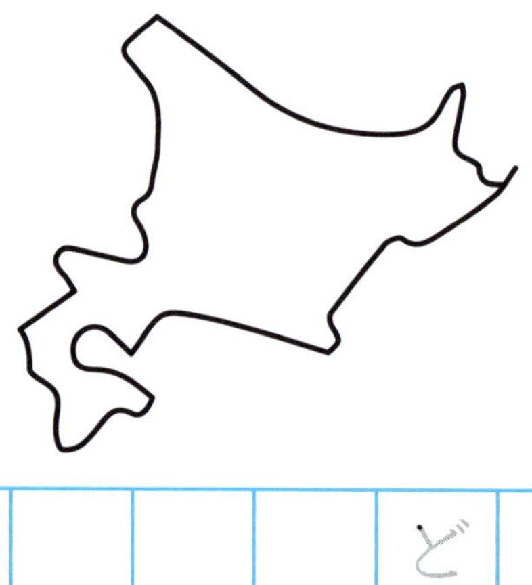

				ど	う
Ho	k	ka	i		u

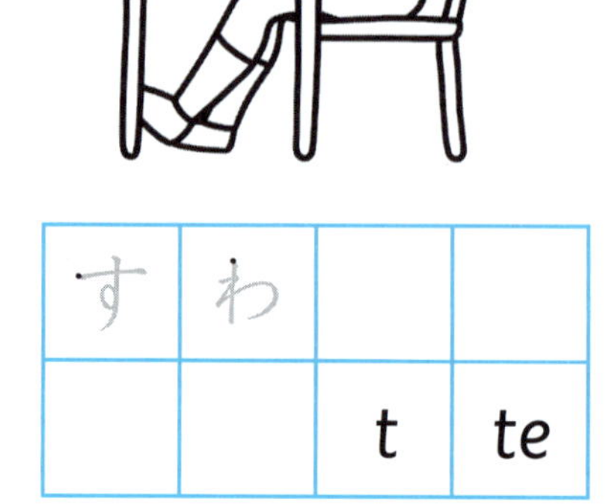

す	わ		
		t	te

When you want to write a long 'o' sound in Japanese, you almost always add the hiragana letter う to the 'o' letter you wish to extend.

The only exceptions to this rule that we need to know for now are:
おおさか – Osaka　　おおきい – big

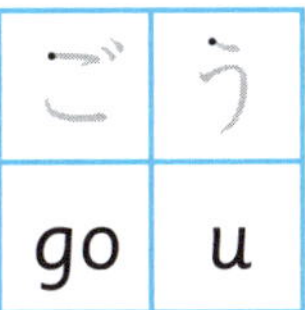
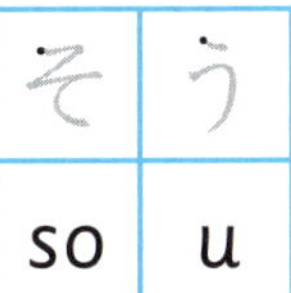
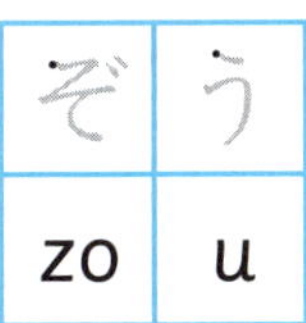
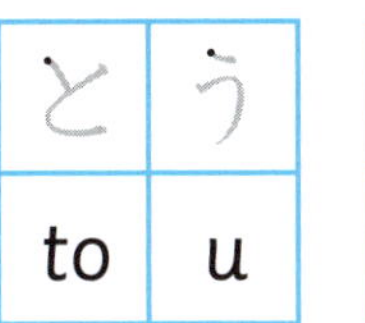

こ	う	ご	う	そ	う	ぞ	う	と	う	ど	う
ko	u	go	u	so	u	zo	u	to	u	do	u

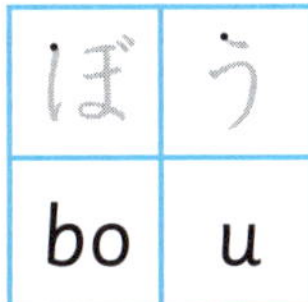
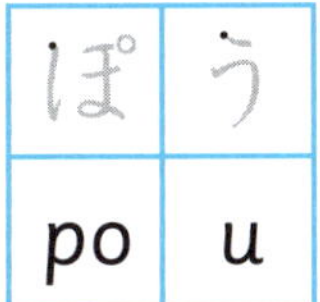
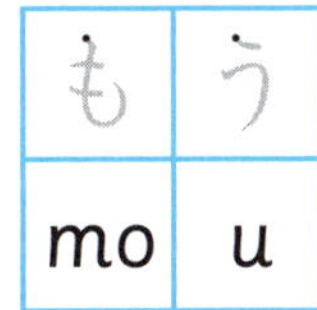
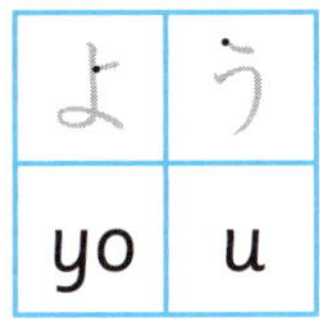

の	う	ほ	う	ぼ	う	ぽ	う	も	う	よ	う	ろ	う
no	u	ho	u	bo	u	po	u	mo	u	yo	u	ro	u

Write the following words using hiragana letters.

o	ha	yo	u	go	za	i	ma	su
good morning								

ha	s	sa	i
8 years old			

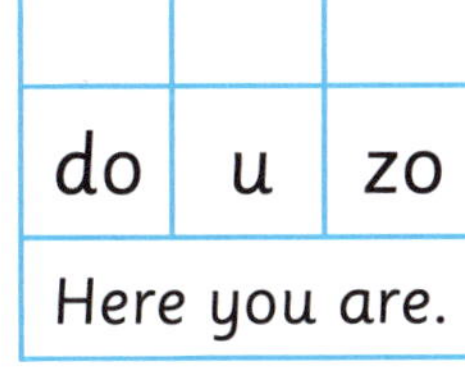
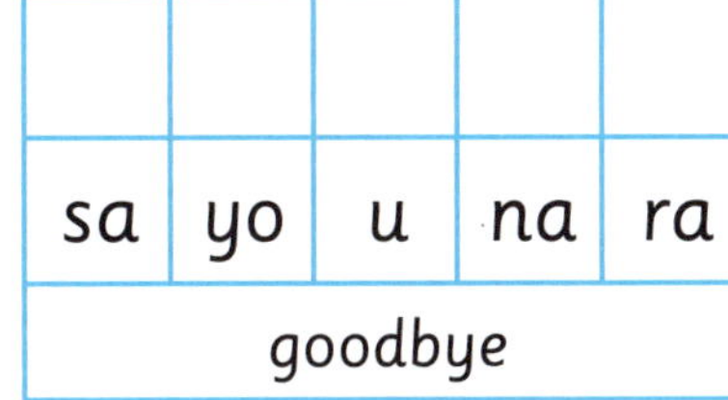

a	ri	ga	to	u
Thank you.				

do	u	zo
Here you are.		

sa	yo	u	na	ra
goodbye				

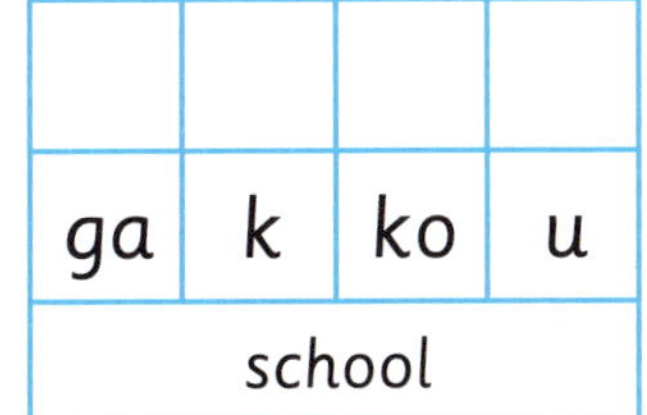
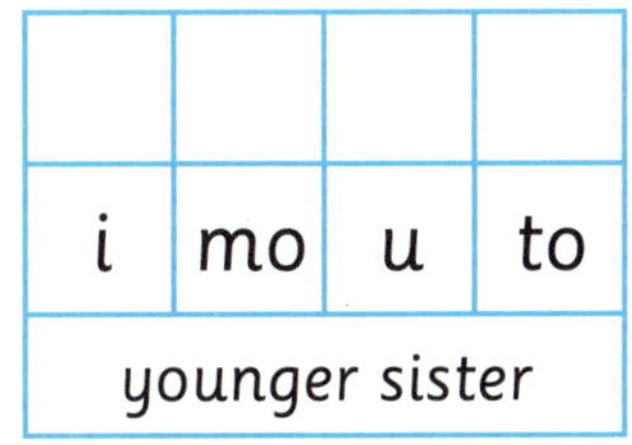

Ho	k	ka	i	do	u
Hokkaido					

ga	k	ko	u
school			

i	mo	u	to
younger sister			

Trace over the Japanese words, then find the one incorrect hiragana letter in each. Cross it out and write its correct replacement in the circle provided. Finally, join your word to the correct picture with a line. Use the vocabulary boxes and wordlists to help you.

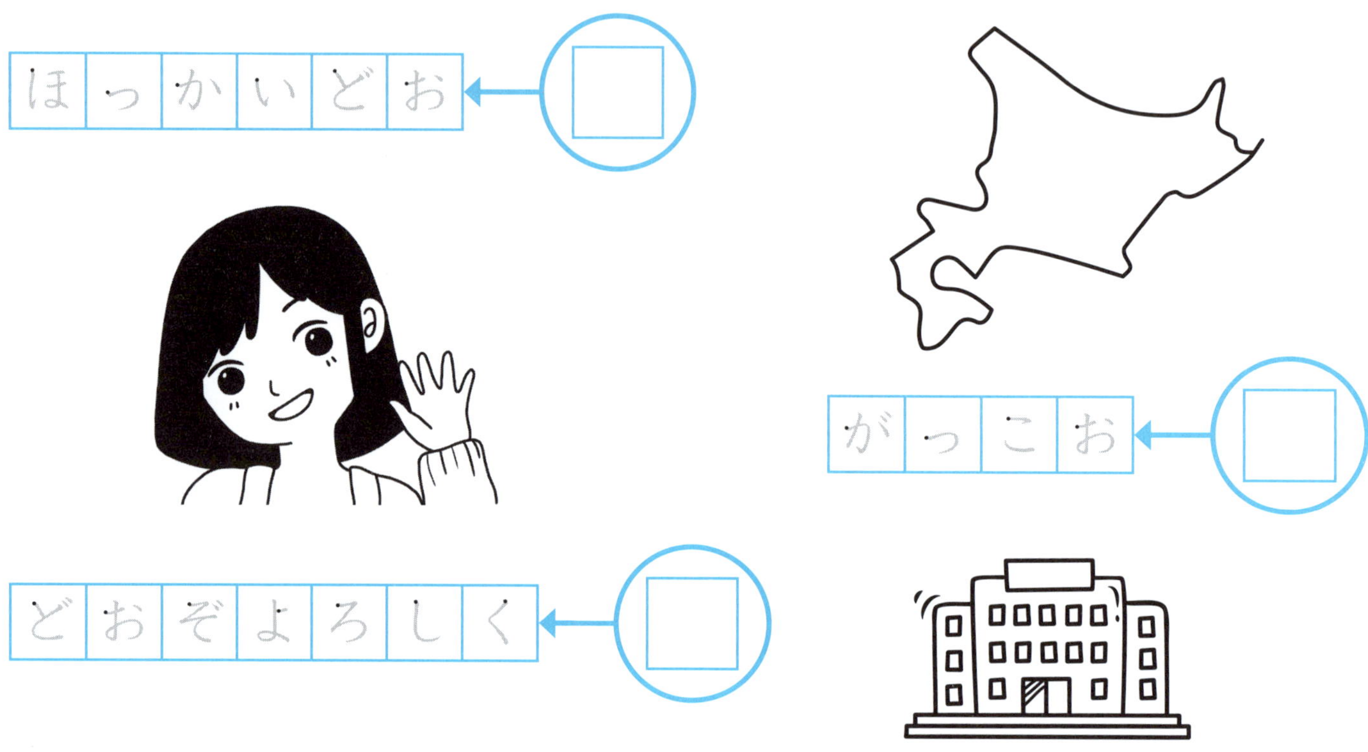

Look at the speech bubble on page 42. How many long 'o' words can you find? List each one, then use them to make your own sentences in the blank boxes provided below. If you don't know what the words mean, use the wordlist at the back of the book or the vocabulary boxes at the top of each Language Lesson to help you.

Long 'o' word:	
Sentence:	

Long 'o' word:	
Sentence:	

Long 'o' word:	
Sentence:	

Long 'o' word:	
Sentence:	

Some hiragana letters have two sounds. They are は and へ. Normally, は says HA, and へ says HE.

BUT …

To write particle WA we use は,
and to write particle E we use へ.

ALSO …

Particle WA (は) is often followed by a Japanese comma, like this:

ぼ	く	は	、

and Japanese sentences end with a Japanese full stop, like this:

で	す	。

Look at these sentences that use particle WA. Trace over the hiragana letters, then write each sentence in romaji and English.

HIRAGANA:	ぼ	く	は	、	た	か	で	す	。
ROMAJI:			wa						
ENGLISH:									

HIRAGANA:	わ	た	し	は	、	は	な	で	す	。
ROMAJI:										
ENGLISH:										

Insert the missing hiragana, romaji or English letters to make the three sentences match.

HIRAGANA:	は		さ				
ROMAJI:		s		i	de	su	.
ENGLISH:	I am ______ years old.						

HIRAGANA:		じ	め				。
ROMAJI:	ha			ma	shi	te	
ENGLISH:	I'm ______ to meet you.						

HIRAGANA:				、	ろ			ん		い			
ROMAJI:	bo	ku	wa	,		ku	ne		se		de	su	.
ENGLISH:	______ am in grade ______.												

HIRAGANA:			ん	に				い			
ROMAJI:	ni	ho			su	n	de		ma	su	.
ENGLISH:	I ______ in ______.										

HIRAGANA:	お		ま		は				で			。
ROMAJI:		na		e		,	na	n		su	ka	
ENGLISH:	______ is your ______?											

HIRAGANA:			さ		で		か	
ROMAJI:	na	n		i		su		.
ENGLISH:	How ______ are you?							

KYA	き	や	き	や	き	や
KYU	き	ゆ	き	ゆ	き	ゆ
KYO	き	よ	き	よ	き	よ

Trace over the correct hiragana blends.

きょ	きゅ	きゃ
KYU		

きゃ	きょ	きゅ
KYA		

きゅ	きょ	きゃ
KYA		

きょ	きゅ	きゃ
KYO		

きゅ	きゃ	きょ
KYU		

きゃ	きょ	きゅ
KYA		

Can you remember these hiragana letters? Write them in the boxes provided.

chi	ke	mi	a	su	ya	ka	na	sa	to	o

so	e	nu	ma	da	yu	ho	ku	fu	te	pe

no	ji	ne	ki	ba	ni	ko	hi	se	tsu	yo

GYA	ぎ	や	ぎ	や	ぎ	や
GYU	ぎ	ゅ	ぎ	ゅ	ぎ	ゅ
GYO	ぎ	ょ	ぎ	ょ	ぎ	ょ

Someone has spilled paint on these hiragana letters and blends. Try to work out which letters or blends they are, then rewrite them in the boxes below with their romaji match. The first one has been done for you.

SHA	し	や	し	や	し	や
SHU	し	ゆ	し	ゆ	し	ゆ
SHO	し	よ	し	よ	し	よ

Fill in the blank boxes (romaji hints are given for missing hiragana blends), then make a sentence with each of the words you have made.

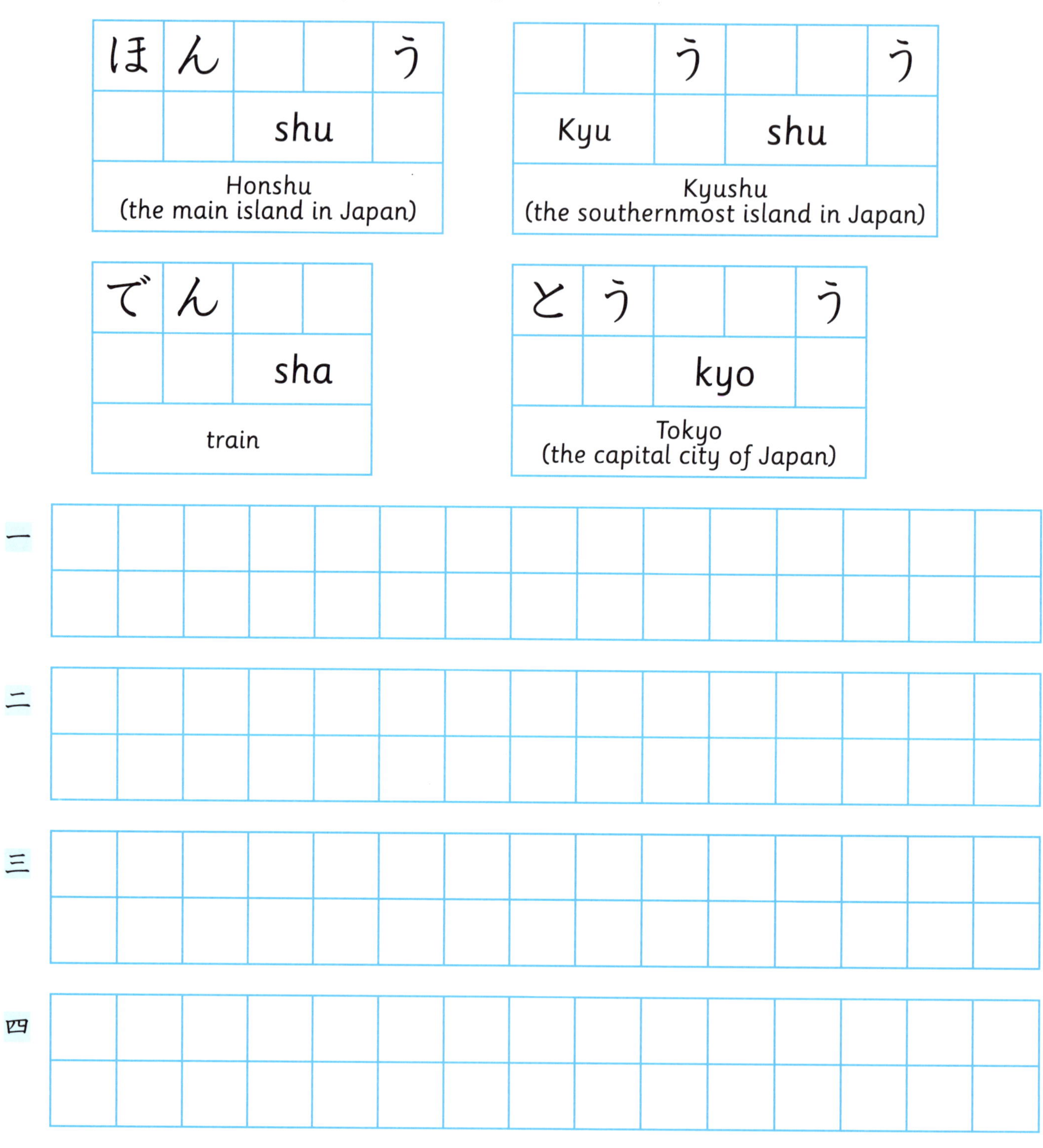

Make up your own sentence in Japanese. Give yourself 5 points for each hiragana blend, small 'tsu', or long 'o' that you use. Give yourself 1 point for each ordinary hiragana letter you use. How many points did you get? ____________

JA	じ	や	じ	や	じ	や
JU	じ	ゆ	じ	ゆ	じ	ゆ
JO	じ	よ	じ	よ	じ	よ

Trace over the hiragana blends, then join them to the matching romaji with a line.

Draw a まる around the hiragana じゃ blends, a しかく around the hiragana じゅ blends and a さんかく around the hiragana じょ blends.

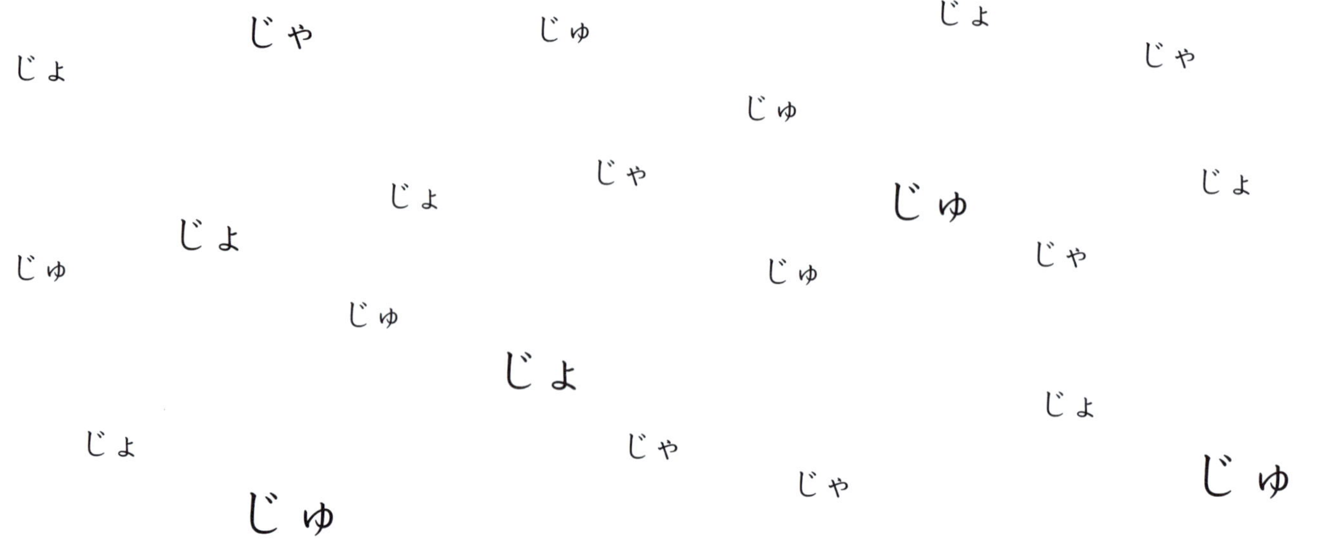

CHA	ち	ゃ	ち	ゃ	ち	ゃ
CHU	ち	ゅ	ち	ゅ	ち	ゅ
CHO	ち	ょ	ち	ょ	ち	ょ

Your school is having a Japanese cultural day and you are going to prepare Japanese green tea（おちゃ）for your fellow students to try. In the frame below, create a sign to promote your green tea stand.

NYA	に	や	に	や	に	や
NYU	に	ゆ	に	ゆ	に	ゆ
NYO	に	よ	に	よ	に	よ

Add one stroke to complete each hiragana blend.

Fill in the blank boxes with the missing hiragana or romaji letters.

		と	う	に		っこ
NYA	JU			NYU	WA	

			ぬ		よ		
MO	U	RE		GYU	NYO	CHO	A

			ちゃ			
HO	SHA	PPO		ME	CHU	SO

HYA	ひ	や	ひ	や	ひ	や
HYU	ひ	ゆ	ひ	ゆ	ひ	ゆ
HYO	ひ	よ	ひ	よ	ひ	よ

There is one mistake in each of these hiragana blends. Circle it, then rewrite the blend correctly in the box provided.

ちゅ	きゃ	ちょ	びょ
cho	gya	cha	hyo
しゅ	きゃ	ひゅ	ちわ
sho	gya	hya	chu
じゅ	ちょ	じゅ	じと
ja	cho	ja	jo
きゅ	じょ	ちゃ	ちゅ
gyu	sho	cho	shu
じあ	ちす	きょ	ぎゅ
ja	chu	kyu	kyu
きょ	ぎゃ	はゅ	ちね
kyu	gyo	hyu	cho

Make up your own sentences in Japanese. Give yourself 5 points for each hiragana blend, small 'tsu', or long 'o' that you use. Give yourself 1 point for each ordinary hiragana letter you use. How many points did you get? ____________

BYA	び	や	び	や	び	や
✍						
✍						
BYU	び	ゆ	び	ゆ	び	ゆ
✍						
✍						
BYO	び	よ	び	よ	び	よ
✍						
✍						

Look at the different ways to write  and .

びゃ	びゅ	びょ
びゃ びゃ びゃ びゃ びゃ びゃ びゃ びゃ びゃ	びゅ びゅ びゅ びゅ びゅ びゅ びゅ びゅ びゅ	びょ びょ びょ びょ びょ びよ びょ ひょ びょ

How many different ways can you write  and ?

びゃ	びゅ	びょ

Can you remember these hiragana blends? Write them in the blank boxes.

kya		cho		byu		kyu		nyu	
sha		gya		ja		nya		gyo	
gyu		nyo		shu		hya		pya	

PYA	ぴ	や	ぴ	や	ぴ	や
PYU	ぴ	ゆ	ぴ	ゆ	ぴ	ゆ
PYO	ぴ	よ	ぴ	よ	ぴ	よ

Join the matching hiragana and romaji letters with a line. Shade the circles with words in あか, with blends in あお, and with single letters in きいろ. One has been done for you.

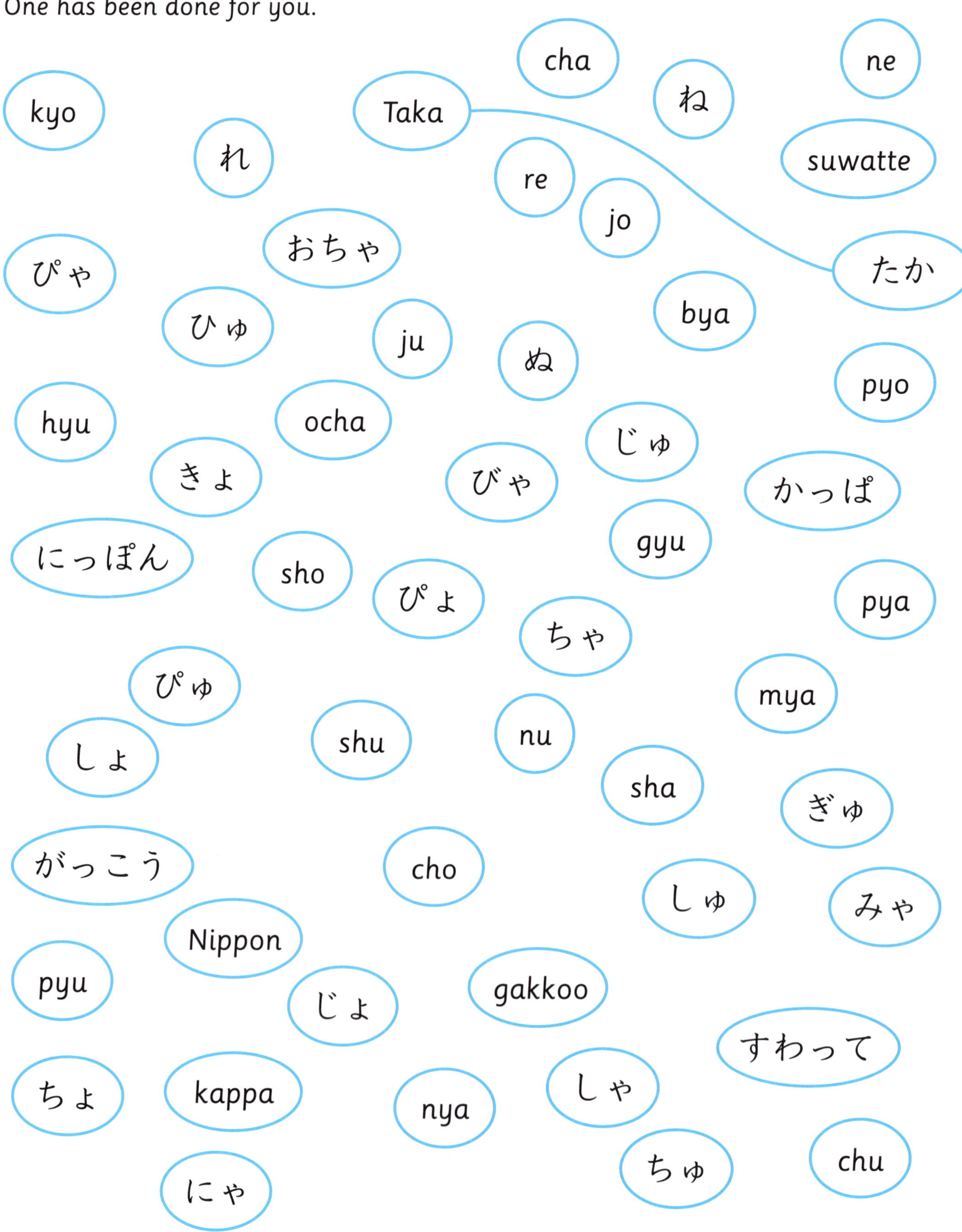

MYA	み	や	み	や	み	や
MYU	み	ゆ	み	ゆ	み	ゆ
MYO	み	よ	み	よ	み	よ

Help the kappa make his way to the pond. Count the number of 'm' hiragana blends you find along the way.

I found: ☐ みゃ blends, ☐ みゅ blends and ☐ みょ blends.

RYA	り	や	り	や	り	や
RYU	り	ゆ	り	ゆ	り	ゆ
RYO	り	よ	り	よ	り	よ

A	I	U	E	O
KA	KI	KU	KE	KO
GA	GI	GU	GE	GO
SA	SHI	SU	SE	SO
ZA	JI	ZU	ZE	ZO
TA	CHI	TSU	TE	TO
DA			DE	DO
NA	NI	NU	NE	NO
HA	HI	FU	HE	HO
BA	BI	BU	BE	BO
PA	PI	PU	PE	PO
MA	MI	MU	ME	MO
YA		YU		YO
RA	RI	RU	RE	RO
WA				PARTICLE O
N				

CONGRATULATIONS!!!

You have completed your hiragana studies.
Test yourself by filling in the hiragana chart. If you can do this without looking, then you have mastered hiragana.
If not, keep on trying!

KYA	KYU	KYO
GYA	GYU	GYO
SHA	SHU	SHO
JA	JU	JO
CHA	CHU	CHO
NYA	NYU	NYO
HYA	HYU	HYO
BYA	BYU	BYO
PYA	PYU	PYO
MYA	MYU	MYO
RYA	RYU	RYO

Choose nine words or phrases from the following list, then write one item in each bingo square. Listen to your teacher to play the game.

はじめまして。	I'm pleased to meet you.	ことし	this year	十七	17
おなまえはなんですか。	What's your name?	にほん	Japan	二十	20
なんさいですか。	How old are you?	アメリカ	America	二十九	29
どこにすんでいますか。	Where do you live?	オーストラリア	Australia	三十一	31
どうぞよろしく。	a greeting used after introducing oneself	ニュー・ジーランド	New Zealand	三十二	32
十さいです。	I'm 10 years old.	とうきょう	Tokyo	三十六	36
五ねんせいです。	I'm in grade 5.	おおさか	Osaka	四十五	45
Hawaii にすんでいます。	I live in Hawaii.	六	6	四十八	48
わたしは、LIZ です。	I am Liz.	八	8	五十	50

LANGUAGE LESSON BINGO		

Choose nine letters, letter groups, or letter blends from the following list, then write one item in each bingo square. Listen to your teacher to play the game.

WRITING LESSON BINGO		

ぬ	nu	たった	tatta	とう	too
ば	ba	きって	kitte	どう	doo
ご	go	みんな	minna	ぼう	boo
ね	ne	ふって	futte	ごう	goo
ぞ	zo	こう	koo	よう	yoo
ぷ	pu	そう	soo	ぼくは	boku wa
げ	ge	ろう	roo	きゃ	kya
ち	chi	どうぞ	doozo	きゅ	kyu
さ	sa	もう	moo	きょ	kyo

Choose nine words or phrases from the following list, then write one item in each bingo square. Listen to your teacher to play the game.

はじめまして。	I'm pleased to meet you.	にほん	Japan	あつい	hot
どこ に すんでいます か。	Where do you live?	おたんじょうび	your birthday	さむい	cold
Sydney に すんでいます。	I live in Sydney.	しずか	quiet	ふゆ	winter
きいて ください。	Please listen.	三がつ	March	なつ	summer
ほん を ひらいて ください。	Please open your book.	十二がつ	December	三十六	36
ほん を とじて ください。	Please close your book.	あたたかい	warm	六十二	62
たんじょうび は、五がつ です。	My birthday is in May.	すずしい	cool	七十九	79
あき が すき です。	I like autumn.	あき	autumn	八十	80
なつ は、あつい です。	Summer is hot.	はる	spring	九十九	99

LANGUAGE LESSON BINGO		

Choose nine letters, letter groups, or letter blends from the following list, then write one item in each bingo square. Listen to your teacher to play the game.

WRITING LESSON BINGO		

ぬ	nu	たった	tatta	しゃ	sha
ぜ	ze	きって	kitte	しゅ	shu
ぎ	gi	みんな	minna	しょ	sho
ね	ne	きゃ	kya	じゃ	ja
め	me	きゅ	kyu	じゅ	ju
ぷ	pu	きょ	kyo	じょ	jo
ゆ	yu	ぎゃ	gya	ちゃ	cha
こう	koo	ぎゅ	gyu	ちゅ	chu
よう	yoo	ぎょ	gyo	ちょ	cho

Choose nine words or phrases from the following list, then write one item in each bingo square. Listen to your teacher to play the game.

六ねんせいです。	I'm in grade 6.	いただきます。	said before eating	はい	yes
にほん に すんでいます。	I live in Japan.	すみません。	Excuse me.	いいえ	no
しずか に して ください。	Please be quiet.	みず を ください。	May I have some water, please?	百	100
みて ください。	Please look.	どうぞ。	Here you are.	二十五	25
ふゆ が すき です。	I like winter.	ごちそうさまでした。	said after eating	四十七	47
なつ は、あつい です。	Summer is hot.	ミルク	milk	五十四	54
やきそば を たべます。	I will eat fried noodles.	ピザ	pizza	六十八	68
なに を たべます か。	What will you eat?	さむい	cold	九十一	91
おちゃ を のみます。	I will drink green tea.	すずしい	cool	九十八	98

LANGUAGE LESSON BINGO		

Choose nine letters, letter groups, or letter blends from the following list, then write one item in each bingo square. Listen to your teacher to play the game.

WRITING LESSON BINGO		

かった	katta	しゃ	sha	にゃ	nya
まった	matta	しゅ	shu	にゅ	nyu
とう	too	しょ	sho	にょ	nyo
きゃ	kya	じゃ	ja	ひゃ	hya
きゅ	kyu	じゅ	ju	ひゅ	hyu
きょ	kyo	じょ	jo	ひょ	hyo
ぎゃ	gya	ちゃ	cha	びゃ	bya
ぎゅ	gyu	ちゅ	chu	びゅ	byu
ぎょ	gyo	ちょ	cho	びょ	byo

Choose nine words or phrases from the following list, then write one item in each bingo square. Listen to your teacher to play the game.

どうぞ よろしく。	said after meeting someone	いただきます。	said before eating	はい	yes
Melbourne に すんでいます。	I live in Melbourne	すみません。	Excuse me.	いいえ	no
みず を のみます。	I will drink water.	なつ	summer	みせ	shops
ホットドッグ を たべます。	I will eat a hot dog.	ふゆ	winter	うみ	sea
それ は、なん です か。	What is that?	あき	autumn	おちゃ	green tea
これ は、ピザ です。	This is pizza.	はる	spring	百	100
どうぶつえん が すき です。	I like the zoo.	これ	this	十六	16
がっこう に いきます。	I go to school.	それ	that	六十二	62
Sue さん は、くるま で いきます。	Sue goes by car.	あれ	that over there	八十五	85

LANGUAGE LESSON BINGO		

Choose nine letters, letter groups, or letter blends from the following list, then write one item in each bingo square. Listen to your teacher to play the game.

WRITING LESSON BINGO		

うって	utte	じゃ	ja	ぴゃ	pya
ふった	futta	じょ	jo	ぴゅ	pyu
もう	moo	ちゅ	chu	ぴょ	pyo
きゃ	kya	ちょ	cho	みゃ	mya
きゅ	kyu	にゅ	nyu	みゅ	myu
ぎゃ	gya	にょ	nyo	みょ	myo
ぎょ	gyo	ひゃ	hya	りゃ	rya
しゃ	sha	ひょ	hyo	りゅ	ryu
しゅ	shu	びゅ	byu	りょ	ryo

HOW MUCH CAN YOU REMEMBER? LL 1-5; WL 1-4

LISTENING

Listen to the teacher, then circle the correct answer.

1	2	3	4	5
America Japan New Zealand	grade 2 grade 6 6 years old	46 28 12	I am Mashte. I'm pleased to meet you. Where do you live?	I'm 9 years old. How old are you? What grade are you in?

6	7	8	9	10
How old are you? I'm pleased to meet you. What's your name?	I'm in grade 4. I live in Yon. I'm 4 years old.	58 100 10	I live in Australia. I live in Japan. I like Japan.	I'm in grade 5. How old are you? Where do you live?

READING

Look at the cards the teacher will show you. Circle the correct answer.

1	2	3	4	5
HO NE SA	SHU PU BU	NU ME NE	SA CHI RA	MI YA SU

6	7	8	9	10
GOU HOU JO	SOU SO KOU	MATTE TATTE TATO	KITTE KOU KATTE	KYA KA KYO

CONGRATULATIONS! You remembered ____ things about Japan and its language.

HOW MUCH CAN YOU REMEMBER? LL 1-10; WL 1-8

LISTENING

Listen to the teacher, then circle the correct answer.

1	2	3	4	5
Japan pencil book	38 March How are you?	99 49 19	Please listen. Please stand. Please sit.	May June December

6	7	8	9	10
your birthday my birthday October	My birthday is in June. I like birthdays. What month is your birthday?	cold hot cool	winter spring autumn	I like summer. Summer is hot. Summer is cold.

READING

Look at the cards the teacher will show you. Circle the correct answer.

1	2	3	4	5
A MA HI	NE HO KE	HOU HO GYO	SHU KYU SHA	KYA GYA GOU

6	7	8	9	10
SHA SHO SO	MATTA TOU CHO	NO NOU JO	SU KYU KU	JA CHA SHO

CONGRATULATIONS! You remembered ____ things about Japan and its language.

HOW MUCH CAN YOU REMEMBER? LL 1-15; WL 1-11

LISTENING

Listen to the teacher, then circle the correct answer.

1	2	3	4	5
no yes what	fried noodles hamburger pizza	water green tea milk	Here you are. Excuse me. May I have some water, please?	Thank you for the food. something said before eating Excuse me.

6	7	8	9	10
eat drink what	I'll drink milk. I'll drink coffee. I'll drink water.	I'll eat pizza. I'll drink coffee. What will you eat?	What will you eat? What will you drink? Do you like water?	Will you drink milk? Do you like milk? I'll drink milk.

READING

Look at the cards the teacher will show you. Circle the correct answer.

1	2	3	4	5
NU NO TO	SHU PO JO	NU NYU NYO	CHU CHI CHO	JO BYU SHU

6	7	8	9	10
CHA JA CHU	HYO NYU NYA	MATTE TATTE TATE	HATTE HYU KATTE	HYA BOU BYO

CONGRATULATIONS! You remembered ______ things about Japan and its language.

HOW MUCH CAN YOU REMEMBER? LL 1-20; WL 1-14

LISTENING

Listen to the teacher, then circle the correct answer.

1	2	3	4	5
this that what	car green tea that over there	bus park shops	Please look. Please stand. Please be quiet.	May July October

6	7	8	9	10
This is a shop. I like shops. I will go to the shops.	Where will you go? What will you eat? I'll have coffee.	I go by plane. I go by bicycle. I go to school.	I will go to the cinema. I will go to the beach. This is the beach.	Kara goes to the shops. Kara goes by bus. Kara goes to the shops by bus.

READING

Look at the cards the teacher will show you. Circle the correct answer.

1	2	3	4	5
KOU KYA KAKKO	NU NYU NOU	HOU HO HYO	SHU KYO JOU	GYU GYA GOU

6	7	8	9	10
SHA SHU SUU	PYA BYU HYU	NO NOU HYO	SHU KYU MYA	RYU RUU RYUU

CONGRATULATIONS! You remembered ______ things about Japan and its language.

WORDLIST – ENGLISH/JAPANESE		
English	**Kanji/Hiragana/Katakana**	**Romaji**
1 · one	一 / いち	I CHI
2 · two	二 / に	NI
3 · three	三 / さん	SA N
4 · four	四 / し / よん	SHI/YO N
5 · five	五 / ご	GO
6 · six	六 / ろく	RO KU
7 · seven	七 / しち / なな	SHI CHI/NA NA
8 · eight	八 / はち	HA CHI
9 · nine	九 / く / きゅう	KU/KYU U
10 · ten	十 / じゅう	JU U
11 · eleven	十一 / じゅう いち	JU U I CHI
12 · twelve	十二 / じゅう に	JU U NI
13 · thirteen	十三 / じゅう さん	JU U SA N
14 · fourteen	十四 / じゅう し / よん	JU U SHI/YO N
15 · fifteen	十五 / じゅう ご	JU U GO
16 · sixteen	十六 / じゅう ろく	JU U RO KU
17 · seventeen	十七 / じゅう しち / なな	JU U SHI CHI/NA NA
18 · eighteen	十八 / じゅう はち	JU U HA CHI
19 · nineteen	十九 / じゅう く / きゅう	JU U KU/KYU U
20 · twenty	二十 / に じゅう	NI JU U
21 · twenty-one	二十一 / に じゅう いち	NI JU U I CHI
30 · thirty	三十 / さん じゅう	SA N JU U
40 · forty	四十 / よん じゅう	YO N JU U
50 · fifty	五十 / ご じゅう	GO JU U
60 · sixty	六十 / ろく じゅう	RO KU JU U
70 · seventy	七十 / しち / なな じゅう	SHI CHI/NA NA JU U
80 · eighty	八十 / はち じゅう	HA CHI JU U
90 · ninety	九十 / きゅう じゅう	KYU U JU U
100 · one hundred	百 / ひゃく	HYA KU
9 o'clock	九じ / くじ	KU JI
Africa	アフリカ	A FU RI KA
am/is/are	です	DE SU
America	アメリカ	A ME RI KA
and also/then	そして	SO SHI TE
April	四がつ / しがつ	SHI GA TSU
Asia	アジア	A JI A

English	Kanji/Hiragana/Katakana	Romaji
at (used with time)	に	NI
August	八がつ / はちがつ	HA CHI GA TSU
Australia	オーストラリア	O O SU TO RA RI A
autumn	あき	A KI
beach/sea	うみ	U MI
bicycle	じてんしゃ	JI TE N SHA
birthday	たんじょうび	TA N JO U BI
bus	バス	BA SU
by (transport)	で	DE
car	くるま	KU RU MA
cinema	えいがかん	E I GA KA N
coffee	コーヒー	KO O HI I
cold	さむい	SA MU I
cool	すずしい	SU ZU SHI I
December	十二がつ / じゅう にがつ	JU U NI GA TSU
drink	のみます	NO MI MA SU
eat	たべます	TA BE MA SU
Europe	ヨーロッパ	YO O RO PPA
Excuse me.	すみません	SU MI MA SE N
February	二がつ / にがつ	NI GA TSU
fried noodles	やきそば	YA KI SO BA
go	いきます	I KI MA SU
green tea	おちゃ	O CHA
greeting used after introducing oneself	どうぞ よろしく	DO U ZO YO RO SHI KU
hamburger	ハンバーガー	HA N BA A GA A
Here you are.	どうぞ	DO U ZO
Hokkaido	ほっかいどう	HO KKA I DO U
Honshu	ほんしゅう	HO N SHU U
hot	あつい	A TSU I
hot dog	ホットドッグ	HO TTO DO GGU
I (used by boys)	ぼく	BO KU
I (used mostly by girls)	わたし	WA TA SHI
I'm pleased to meet you	はじめまして	HA JI ME MA SHI TE
in (a season)	に	NI
January	一がつ / いちがつ	I CHI GA TSU

English	Kanji/Hiragana/Katakana	Romaji
Japan	にほん / にっぽん	NI HO N / NI PPO N
juice	ジュース	JU U SU
July	七がつ / しちがつ	SHI CHI GA TSU
June	六がつ / ろくがつ	RO KU GA TSU
Kyushu	きゅうしゅう	KYU U SHU U
like	すき	SU KI
March	三がつ / さんがつ	SA N GA TSU
May	五がつ / ごがつ	GO GA TSU
milk	ミルク	MI RU KU
(my) birthday	たんじょうび	TA N JO U BI
(my) name	なまえ	NA MA E
name	なまえ	NA MA E
New Zealand	ニュー・ジーランド	NYU U JI I RA N DO
no	いいえ	I I E
North America	きた アメリカ	KI TA A ME RI KA
November	十一がつ / じゅう いちがつ	JU U I CHI GA TSU
October	十がつ / じゅうがつ	JU U GA TSU
Osaka	おおさか	O O SA KA
park	こうえん	KO U E N
particle wa	は	WA
pizza	ピザ	PI ZA
plane	ひこうき	HI KO U KI
please	ください	KU DA SA I
Please be quiet.	しずか に して ください。	SHI ZU KA NI SHI TE KU DA SA I
Please close your book.	ほん を とじて ください。	HO N O TO JI TE KU DA SA I
Please listen.	きいて ください。	KI I TE KU DA SA I
Please look.	みて ください。	MI TE KU DA SA I
Please open your book.	ほん を ひらいて ください。	HO N O HI RA I TE KU DA SA I
Please sit.	すわって ください。	SU WA TTE KU DA SA I
Please stand.	たって ください。	TA TTE KU DA SA I
question particle	か	KA
said after eating	ごちそうさまでした。	GO CHI SO U SA MA DE SHI TA
said before eating	いただきます。	I TA DA KI MA SU

English	Kanji/Hiragana/Katakana	Romaji
sandwich	サンドイッチ	SA N DO I TCHI
school	がっこう	GA KKO U
sea/beach	うみ	U MI
September	九がつ / くがつ	KU GA TSU
Shikoku	しこく	SHI KO KU
shop(s)	みせ	MI SE
South America	みなみ アメリカ	MI NA MI A ME RI KA
spring	はる	HA RU
summer	なつ	NA TSU
tea (green)	おちゃ	O CHA
teacher	せんせい	SE N SE I
Thank you for the food. (said after eating)	ごちそうさまでした。	GO CHI SO U SA MA DE SHI TA
that	それ	SO RE
that over there	あれ	A RE
this	これ	KO RE
this year	ことし	KO TO SHI
to (a place)	に	NI
Tokyo	とうきょう	TO U KYO U
warm	あたたかい	A TA TA KA I
water	みず	MI ZU
water monster	かっぱ	KA PPA
what	なに / なん	NA NI / NA N
what month	なんがつ	NA N GA TSU
where	どこ	DO KO
winter	ふゆ	FU YU
yes	はい	HA I
(your) birthday	おたんじょうび	O TA N JO U BI
(your) name	おなまえ	O NA MA E
zoo	どうぶつえん	DO U BU TSU E N

SENTENCE PATTERN LIST – ENGLISH/JAPANESE		
English	**Kanji/Hiragana/Katakana**	**Romaji**
I am ☺☺☺ years old.	☺☺☺ さい です。	☺☺☺ SA I DE SU.
I am in grade ☺☺☺.	☺☺☺ ねんせい です。	☺☺☺ NE N SE I DE SU.
I am ☺☺☺.	☺☺☺ です。	☺☺☺ DE SU.
I go to ☺☺☺.	☺☺☺ に いきます。	☺☺☺ NI I KI MA SU.
I like ☺☺☺.	☺☺☺ が すき です。	☺☺☺ GA SU KI DE SU.
I live in ☺☺☺.	☺☺☺ に すんでいます。	☺☺☺ NI SU N DE I MA SU.
I'll drink ☺☺☺.	☺☺☺ を のみます。	☺☺☺ O NO MI MA SU.
May I have ☺☺☺?	☺☺☺ を ください。	☺☺☺ O KU DA SA I.
My birthday is in ☺☺☺.	たんじょうび は、☺☺☺ がつ です。	TA N JO U BI WA, ☺☺☺ GA TSU DE SU.
This is ☺☺☺.	これ は、☺☺☺ です。	KO RE WA, ☺☺☺ DE SU.
What is this?	これ は、なん です か。	KO RE WA, NA N DE SU KA.
What month is ☺☺☺?	☺☺☺ は、なん がつ です か。	☺☺☺ WA, NA N GA TSU DE SU KA.
What will you drink?	なに を のみます か。	NA NI O NO MI MA SU KA.
Where will you go?	どこ に いきます か。	DO KO NI I KI MA SU KA.
Will you drink ☺☺☺?	☺☺☺ を のみます か。	☺☺☺ O NO MI MA SU KA.
☺A☺ is ☺B☺	☺A☺ は、☺B☺ です。	☺A☺ WA, ☺B☺ DE SU.

HIRAGANA CHART

あ A	い I	う U	え E	お O
か KA	き KI	く KU	け KE	こ KO
が GA	ぎ GI	ぐ GU	げ GE	ご GO
さ SA	し SHI	す SU	せ SE	そ SO
ざ ZA	じ JI	ず ZU	ぜ ZE	ぞ ZO
た TA	ち CHI	つ TSU	て TE	と TO
だ DA			で DE	ど DO
な NA	に NI	ぬ NU	ね NE	の NO
は HA	ひ HI	ふ FU	へ HE	ほ HO
ば BA	び BI	ぶ BU	べ BE	ぼ BO
ぱ PA	ぴ PI	ぷ PU	ぺ PE	ぽ PO
ま MA	み MI	む MU	め ME	も MO
や YA		ゆ YU		よ YO
ら RA	り RI	る RU	れ RE	ろ RO
わ WA				を particle O
ん N				

HIRAGANA COMBINATION CHART

きゃ	きゅ	きょ
kya	kyu	kyo
ぎゃ	ぎゅ	ぎょ
gya	gyu	gyo
しゃ	しゅ	しょ
sha	shu	sho
じゃ	じゅ	じょ
ja	ju	jo
ちゃ	ちゅ	ちょ
cha	chu	cho
にゃ	にゅ	にょ
nya	nyu	nyo
ひゃ	ひゅ	ひょ
hya	hyu	hyo
びゃ	びゅ	びょ
bya	byu	byo
ぴゃ	ぴゅ	ぴょ
pya	pyu	pyo
みゃ	みゅ	みょ
mya	myu	myo
りゃ	りゅ	りょ
rya	ryu	ryo

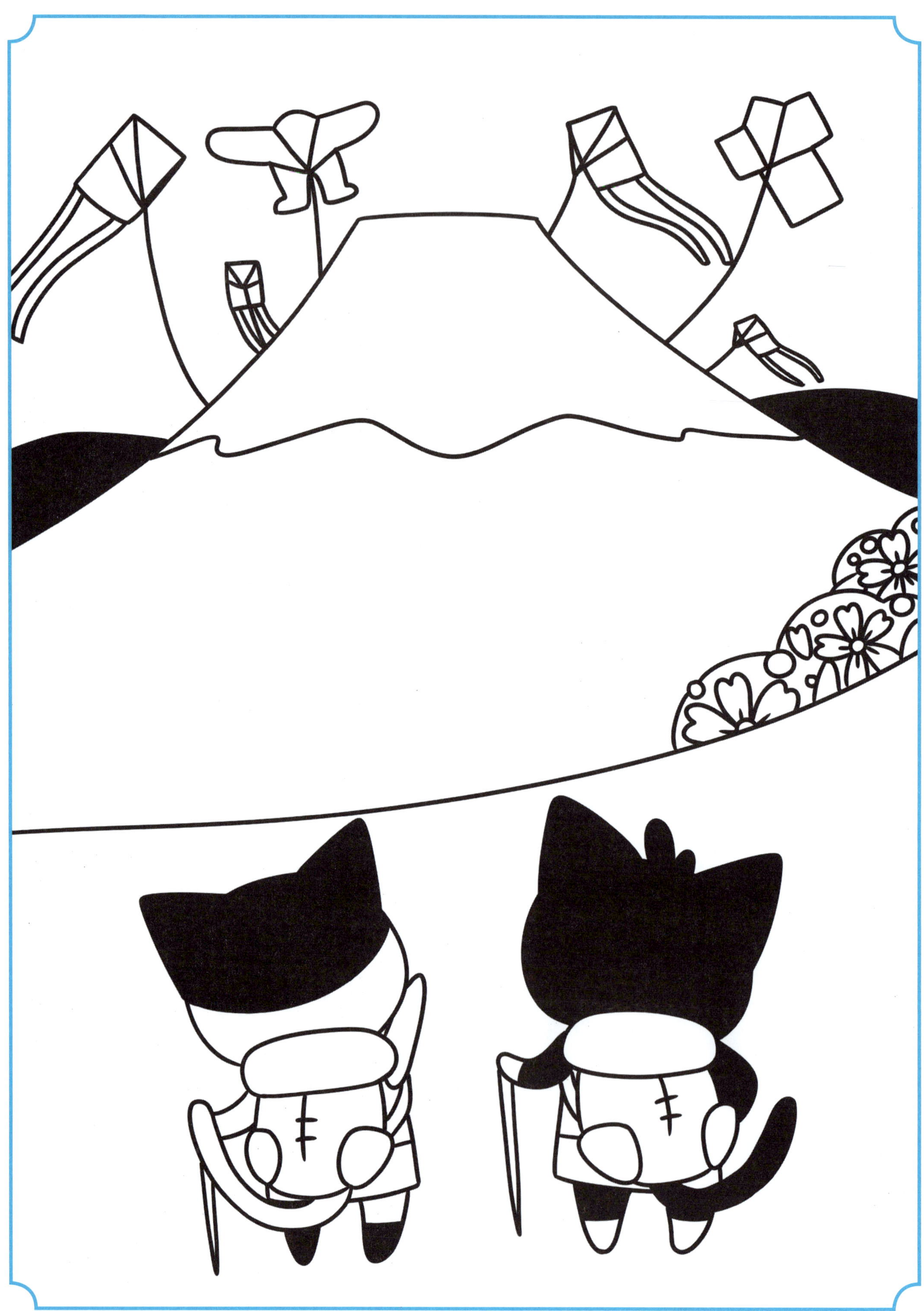

